IMPACT TECHNIQUES

IN THE CLASSROOM

BY THE SAME AUTHOR

Books

Fascicules d'Impact en classe: activités éducatives pour développer toutes les intelligences (9 *numéros*), volume 1: *niveau primaire*, Québec, Éditions Académie Impact, 2002.

Techniques d'Impact pour grandir: illustrations pour développer l'intelligence émotionnelle chez les enfants, Québec, Éditions Académie Impact, 2000.

Techniques d'Impact pour grandir: illustrations pour développer l'intelligence émotionnelle chez les adolescents, Québec, Éditions Académie Impact, 2000.

Techniques d'Impact pour grandir: illustrations pour développer l'intelligence émotionnelle chez les adultes, Québec, Éditions Académie Impact, 2000.

Cures de rajeunissement pour vos relations sexuelles, Québec, Éditions Académie Impact, 2000.

Mille feuilles à l'encre et à la crème: 500 lettres et suggestions pour les événements heureux, avec la collaboration de Célyn Bonnet, Québec, Éditions Académie Impact, 1998.

Mille feuilles à l'encre et à la crème: 500 lettres et suggestions pour les événements malheureux, avec la collaboration de Célyn Bonnet, Québec, Éditions Académie Impact, 1998.

Techniques d'Impact en psychothérapie, relation d'aide et santé mentale, second edition, Québec, Éditions Académie Impact, 2002 (©1997).

Eye Movement Integration Therapy: The Comprehensive Guide, Carmarthen, Wales, UK, Crown House Publishing Limited, 2003.

Techniques d'Impact en classe, Québec, Éditions Académie Impact, 2001.

Roy, Édith and Danie Beaulieu *Techniques d'Impact au préscolaire*, Québec, Éditions Académie Impact, 2004.

Development workbooks

100 trucs pour améliorer vos relations avec les enfants, Third edition, Québec, Éditions Académie Impact, 2002 (©1999).

100 trucs pour améliorer vos relations avec les ados, Third edition, Québec, Éditions Académie Impact, 2002 (©1999).

Découvrez l'héritage de vos mémoires, Québec, Éditions Académie Impact, 2001.

La fatigue et l'épuisement, Québec, Éditions Académie Impact, 2000.

Devenir un meilleur leader dans un groupe de thérapie, Québec, Éditions Académie Impact, 1998.

L'Art de semer, Québec, Éditions Académie Impact, 2003.

Manuel d'entretien de la vie amoureuse, Québec, Éditions Académie Impact, 2003.

Relations interpersonnelles de 0/10 à 10/10, Québec, Éditions Académie Impact, 2000.

Danie Beaulieu, PhD

IMPACT TECHNIQUES
IN THE CLASSROOM

Crown House Publishing Limited
www.crownhouse.co.uk

First published as *Techniques d'Impact en classe* by Éditions Académie Impact in 2001.

English paperback edition published by

Crown House Publishing Ltd
Crown Buildings, Bancyfelin, Carmarthen, Wales, SA33 5ND, UK
www.crownhouse.co.uk

and

Crown House Publishing Company LLC
4 Berkeley Street, 1st Floor, Norwalk, CT 06850, USA
www.CHPUS.com

British Library of Cataloguing-in-Publication Data
A catalogue entry for this book is available from the British Library.

International Standard Book Number
1904424554

Library of Congress Control Number
2004111431

Printed and bound in the UK by
Gomer Press
Llandysul

If the techniques presented in this book prove useful to you, enabling you to bring more efficiency and pleasure to your work as a teacher, then you need only "pay it forward".

Instructions can be found in the film of the same name.

TABLE OF CONTENTS

The Quick Reference Matrix is designed to enable you to find appropriate techniques and tips for the particular issues you need to explore or resolve.

Techniques

Issues	1	2	3	4	5	6	7	8	9	10	11	12	13	14	15	16	17	18	19	20	21	22	23	24	25	26	27	28	29	30	31	32	33	34	35	36	37	38	39
Absenteeism																																							
Self-assertiveness															✓																			✓	✓				
Aptitudes for success (reinforcement)																				✓							✓	✓							✓	✓	✓		✓
Attention and concentration	✓				✓	✓	✓		✓	✓				✓		✓		✓		✓			✓				✓	✓											
Attention and receptiveness to others (interpersonal relationships)						✓																					✓										✓	✓	
Negative attitude toward school						✓				✓		✓	✓					✓		✓		✓																	
Self-discipline			✓		✓	✓	✓		✓					✓							✓	✓				✓			✓				✓	✓		✓			✓
Civility and politeness						✓															✓		✓	✓														✓	
Group cohesion and bonding	✓				✓	✓						✓		✓															✓	✓	✓				✓				
Teacher–student bonding				✓				✓																									✓						
Compulsive achievement													✓													✓	✓												
Self-confidence		✓	✓																														✓						
Conflicts and rivalry																																							
Self-awareness and expressing feelings						✓			✓			✓	✓							✓						✓					✓				✓				✓
Assignment instructions			✓			✓	✓			✓								✓																		✓			
Drug and alcohol use									✓		✓									✓	✓																		
Cutting class																																							
Deprecation																✓							✓																
Learning problems and poor grades	✓										✓			✓				✓	✓								✓	✓						✓	✓	✓			✓
Distractions and agitation					✓									✓		✓					✓	✓							✓										
Class dynamics	✓				✓	✓		✓					✓		✓		✓														✓			✓		✓	✓	✓	
Failure																			✓	✓														✓					
Empathy						✓								✓																✓	✓						✓		
Self-esteem		✓																		✓																			
Exams (stress)										✓											✓																		
Participation in class			✓				✓								✓		✓								✓	✓	✓								✓				
Harmful influences										✓	✓									✓																			
Guiding students to aid resources																				✓												✓							
Parents (meeting with)																																							
Perseverance																						✓												✓	✓	✓			
Worries and anxiety	✓			✓	✓			✓	✓											✓			✓																✓
Rejection		✓	✓	✓													✓			✓			✓		✓														
Promoting student responsibility															✓																			✓					
School assignments (making an effort, planning, prioritizing)				✓		✓							✓									✓		✓	✓	✓	✓		✓					✓	✓	✓			✓
Tolerance														✓																				✓			✓		
Disruptions															✓										✓														

Please note that the numbers are those assigned to the techniques, except for the tips, in which case page numbers are expressly indicated.

Techniques

40	41	42	43	44	45	46	47	48	49	50	51	52	53	54	55	56	57	58	59	60	61	62	63	64	65	66	67	68	69	70	71	72	73	74	75	76	77	78	79	80	81	82	83	84	85	86	87	88	
										✓							✓																																
																																																	TIP p.67
				✓			✓				✓	✓												✓							✓	✓						✓	✓										TIPS p.49, 127, 155
✓	✓		✓	✓						✓		✓		✓		✓	✓																					✓		✓						✓			TIPS p.69, 175
				✓							✓					✓				✓									✓						✓		✓												TIPS p.87, 119, 169, 171
				✓				✓														✓																											
												✓					✓																															
				✓				✓				✓												✓													✓											
				✓								✓								✓								✓							✓												✓		TIPS p.65, 87, 97, 101, 119, 169, 171
									✓			✓	✓				✓	✓								✓					✓					✓													TIPS p.101, 141
				✓					✓																																								
																														✓		✓				✓													TIP p.97
						✓	✓	✓				✓							✓			✓				✓	✓							✓															
																							✓	✓		✓	✓				✓	✓	✓				✓												TIPS p.69, 105, 123, 139, 169, 171
✓												✓																																					TIPS p.97, 117, 121, 165
				✓							✓									✓	✓																												
							✓	✓	✓																																							
												✓																✓										✓		✓									
	✓		✓			✓	✓		✓	✓	✓	✓			✓																									✓									TIP p.141
	✓														✓																																		
				✓																								✓							✓														TIPS p.87, 97, 121, 165, 169
																																					✓												
																																		✓															TIPS p.105, 119, 123, 169
																	✓							✓		✓	✓																						TIP p.119
																																		✓															TIPS p.127, 155
✓			✓		✓							✓					✓		✓		✓	✓													✓													TIPS p.101, 105
											✓					✓																																
						✓					✓																✓															✓						TIP p.123
																										✓	✓													✓	✓							
											✓				✓							✓	✓													✓	✓											
		✓		✓			✓		✓		✓											✓	✓	✓																					✓			
				✓														✓	✓		✓							✓										✓						✓	TIP p.141
																						✓	✓	✓								✓	✓													TIP p.97
✓	✓		✓	✓													✓	✓			✓	✓									✓			✓	✓		✓	✓										
																											✓									✓												
	✓										✓																				✓			✓	✓									✓				

ACKNOWLEDGMENTS

I have a soft spot for pearls—I really love them. Mainly for their story of succeeding to develop such beauty, strength and brilliance from such simple materials and the labor of time. Fine pearls are rare and much sought after.

I had the opportunity of meeting one, a real one. She is called Marie-Claude Malenfant. She completed a doctorate in French literature at the University of Clermont-Ferrand, in France, and a post-doctoral fellowship at McGill University in Quebec. Marie-Claude wrote these pages for me. I gave her the cassettes containing a description of each of the techniques and she knew how to put them into words with great tact and competence. Her love of words, coupled with the perfectionist nature she has gained through experience, has given her composition clarity, simplicity, and refinement. I feel truly privileged to have been able to benefit from her professionalism.

I would also like to thank Marianne Tremblay for the book design. I greatly appreciate her ideas, expertise, efficiency, and availability.

Nadia Berghella did the illustrations in this volume. She is a great artist in my opinion and it was a pleasure to work with her.

Finally, I must offer my appreciation to the teachers and principals to whom I have provided training on Impact Techniques in the Classroom. Their varied questions and comments enabled me to add greater realism and richness to this book.

PREFACE

I published the *Impact Techniques Manual*, in 1997, for interventions in psychotherapy, the helping professions, and mental health; that was my first bestseller. Whatever the audience or the profession I present them to, and in any setting, Impact Techniques are always received enthusiastically, adopted immediately, and then applied in the field with success. The positive feedback that I receive and the specific requests formulated for some years by teachers and education professionals have prompted me to draft techniques specific to the universe that is the classroom. The reason I speak of a universe is that the classroom is a microcosm in itself, a heterogeneous group of identities, both defined and developing. It is an organism that does a self-search when one of its members is missing, and sometimes, as you know, a stubborn, obstinate entity that you consider almost as a foreign body …

When consulting the index of the Impact Techniques, you will note that many of the techniques relate to classroom management, others focus on a specific behavioral or attitude problem with a student, others still are designed to offer support in dealing with a difficulty a young person is going through. However varied they are, all—without exception—contribute to nourishing and developing the emotional intelligence of your students. Whichever technique you use, whether it addresses the group or an individual student, all of my techniques reinforce one or several emotional aptitudes, be it self-control (resisting urges, delaying the satisfaction of desires), empathy (recognizing the feelings of another, understanding their feelings, and building better relationship with them) and the ability to motivate oneself (perseverance, enthusiasm for work or in actions). In the context of today, when the majority of young people spend more time at school than at home and now that teachers have a much greater feeling than before of having to "raise" their students, this aspect of learning about life plays a significant role in the classroom, alongside more formal teaching of the subject matter. Yet, you have to simultaneously educate many students on both the intellectual and emotional levels; you have little time, energy or desire to plunge into an in-depth therapy session. Your approach should therefore be directed towards results; in the context of your classroom, this means that you should quickly favor the development of feelings of confidence, well-being, acceptance, and tolerance. You then need to maintain this clean and motivating learning environment, so that each student feels welcomed and respected, and so that they can learn to welcome and respect one another.

How do you go about creating a collective space, arousing the desire to participate within *every* student and thus establish the best conditions for transmitting knowledge? The Impact Techniques that I suggest diversify the means of creating such an environment, using objects, proposing experiments, suggesting movements and offering some tips—that is, more succinct, rapidly applicable techniques, which set about reinforcing the dynamics and synergy of the group. In reading the following pages, you will quickly identify the type of intervention with which you feel most comfortable, but I would also ask you to consider the needs of your group as well as its "nature". You may well question whether a technique that works well with an elementary school class made up mostly of girls, would produce such powerful effects with adolescents at the end of high school education. Besides the standard applications, you will occasionally have to adapt a technique more specifically to your environment or try it out with a young person you know before implementing it with your group or with an individual student.

Remember that the only way to become truly at ease with your interventions is to dare, or maybe even, to dare without knowing the precise results that will be achieved. Your classroom, as I said earlier, is an organism, an entity in its own right, whose reactions can't be easily predicted. Each young person you encounter also has their own way of interpreting your approach, which may vary from mistrust to complete confidence, depending on the type of relationships you have established with him, what he has learned to believe etc. Bear in mind that the important thing isn't so much to multiply the number of techniques you use, but rather to ensure that you frequently benefit from the ones that you have used effectively, through repeated reminders and brief allusions. Accordingly, I recommend a little flexibility and inventiveness in the application of these techniques and a detached attitude in … the lions den!

INTRODUCTION

You teach. Therefore, at one time or another, you have wished with all your heart that your students would suddenly develop a spontaneous, automatic, and lasting ability to record everything you teach them: instructions, the principles of living with others, and the subject matter that you teach. Often, upon reflection, it's not so much the lectures on the subject matter that you find yourself repeating again and again, but rather everything relating to the exhausting and never-ending task of classroom management. You remain continuously on the lookout to ensure discipline within the group and watch even more closely certain students who need to be regularly—and so often!—told to be quiet or whose attention needs to be re-activated at regular intervals. You have also developed a hypervigilance to channel the effervescent energy of certain "free electrons" who must constantly be brought back to order—who move, talk, giggle, get up, and walk around ...

In short, many teachers have admitted to me that they feel that they spend the majority of the lesson time doing anything and everything but teaching. With *Impact Techniques in the Classroom*, I offer you a variety of activities to be done as a group or on a one-on-one basis (and a few with the help of the parents) that will allow you to devote more time to teaching, all the while saving your energy and quickly capturing the attention of your students.

Impact Techniques will allow you to make progress toward these objectives through simple and easily applicable activities. They've been designed to exploit and apply the current knowledge about how the brain and memory function. Using an Impact Technique is like giving your teaching efforts a sort of learning amplifier, which multiplies the anchors in the students' minds, allowing them to integrate new knowledge (whether intellectual or emotional) more quickly, more deeply, and with greater intensity. The effectiveness of Impact Techniques—which, as you will see, is immediately noticeable in the classroom—is a result of a combination of many factors. The underlying principle is that, because these techniques are not limited to verbal language and because they appeal to many senses, the information that they transmit lodges in several areas of the brain and thus constitutes a global message that is loaded with possibilities for recall.

In addition, by using objects, images, and movements, these techniques target the student's implicit memory—the form of memory that decodes information through intuition and experience. This form of memory functions outside of the person's conscious control, as demonstrated in a recent experiment involving subjects who had undergone a resection of the *corpus callosum*, the thoroughfare that assures communication between the two cerebral hemispheres (a procedure that is usually performed to control severe epilepsy).[1] With the aid of an apparatus that projects an image to only one hemisphere, the researchers were able to observe that, in fact, as expected, an image perceived by the left hemisphere—which dominates on the verbal level—can be clearly described by the patient. On the other hand, and rather more surprisingly, images presented to and perceived by the right hemisphere—that of musical language, images, and emotions—pass unnoticed. The right brain isn't able to verbally translate that which it has nevertheless registered. Since it is the left brain that responds, the patient would even affirm that he has not seen the image! However, when asked to point with his left hand (which is controlled by the right brain) to an object that represents the projected image, his fingers are lead in the right direction, to the great surprise of the left brain, which has no idea at all why he is making that gesture!

These results indicate that people possess many different channels of learning and that, to obtain the best possible results in a student, all of his faculties must be recruited, as much to the process of assimilation of information as to its expression. Too often, our classroom teaching exploits principally, if not uniquely, the verbal zone of the brain. Some teachers feel as though they have tried everything … when they have *said* everything. However, Bessel van der Kolk, an American psychiatrist and researcher specializing in memory, maintains that only a small percentage of our learning is based on explicit memory, either through language or rational thought.[2]

This book, then, offers tools to develop the implicit dimension of your teaching and thus expand your efficiency by soliciting the maximum from your students' cerebral radars. Let's have a look at this in a bit more detail.

From the known toward the unknown

It has been shown that the memory more easily retains new information that contains elements that are already known, as opposed to material that is completely unconnected to the person's stock of knowledge. For example, if you possess no rudimentary knowledge in the field, a speech given by an enthusiastically passionate astrophysicist on the powers of quantum physics would give you a feeling of wandering in a dense fog. Similarly, it's vital to allow the mind of the student to rely on what he already knows if you would like him to understand what you are explaining. Consequently, many Impact Techniques use objects that serve as recognizable aid to thought and discussion.

Thus, using a lamp and a light bulb, you will be able to help your students to create favorable conditions for better attention and concentration by themselves. Rather than simply repeating or imploring, "Now please concentrate", direct this exercise by asking them to comment on the following different stages (it is particularly important to simultaneously do all the actions described in front of the class): What happens if the bulb is not screwed into the lamp? And what if the lamp isn't plugged into the electrical outlet? When the switch is in the off position? Even if the bulb possesses all the potential energy to provide a source of light, it cannot do so if one of these conditions has not been met. Next, draw a parallel between the electric bulb and the student's mental "light bulb"—the one that lights up inside each student to help him or her understand what is being taught in class. Like the electric light bulb, the comprehension process is sometimes interrupted by small problems. For example, despite all its capacity, that internal light bulb can't light up if the student's mind is not plugged into what the teacher is saying, when the student's motivation is in the "off" position, or when the method for doing the assignment is not appropriate for what is requested (in other words, the internal light bulb is not screwed in properly). Encourage each student to ask himself if one or more of these problems is preventing him from "lighting up" on what is being taught. Then you need to guide the student in his search for solutions so that his intellectual light bulb may—from then on—provide optimal light. However, a significant part of this solution is already sensed, as the student *knows* how to make the bulb work.

In an exercise of this nature, the demonstration—using the object selected to support the deductions of the student—is directly responsible for the impact that the comparison to his own behavior will have on the student. The principles that he observes in action will appear just as valid when he applies them to his own case, because he has discovered that the two situations are analogous. Furthermore, by firmly anchoring a new piece of information to already acquired knowledge, you will be recruiting the student's competence and making it more likely that the new information will be remembered.

Let's take the number 911 as an example, the number that is already known as the number to dial in emergencies. If I told you that you could reach a new service at 119, which has the opposite role of the former, that is, to take nonurgent calls for help, you would remember this new code immediately and for some time. The more the first piece of knowledge is integrated and mastered, the better and quicker the second can be integrated and mastered.

When you teach, you have the choice of using one of the two receptacles in the minds of your students: one that contains known and mastered information and another for knowledge to be acquired. When you deposit a new piece of information in the first receptacle, it is retained because it catches on other similar information as it goes by. But when you pour new information into the receptacle of the unknown, many, many repetitions are needed to record and integrate that new information with the student's retrievable knowledge.

Be interesting

Can you remember the color of the house number plaque of your second neighbor on the left? Hard, isn't it? Why? Because it doesn't interest you. Memory functions according to the principle of interest: it retains information that is related to something of particular interest. It can hardly function otherwise in the child or teenager that you are teaching! Thus, to aid the "absent-minded dreamer"-type student to develop her ability to concentrate, you can explain to her how and why and when she needs to concentrate, and then wait and see how well this discussion produces results. However, as this discussion probably doesn't interest her very much, there is little chance that the message will get through. There is a much more productive way of going about things: Give her a magazine, the main subject of which interests her and ask if she has a greater tendency to linger over the ads or the articles. Clearly, when too much attention is given to the advertisements, we bypass the essence (the information contained in the articles). Then compare her behavior at school with reading the magazine, making a parallel between the ads and her distractions in class, then between her studious attention and the leading articles. It will then be possible, as you move between the rows during an exercise, to discreetly ask if she is turning the pages of the ads or if she is reading the articles. In recalling to her memory all that you discussed, you enable her to re-center herself quickly and get her concentration focused on the work she needs to do. Thus, instead of using a negative message—like reminding her that she is again wandering off into dreamland—you refer to something that she likes, making her feel less threatened and more respected.

An image is always more powerful than a word

An image possesses the ability to express a lot of information in a concentrated and resonant way rather than a long explanation. That's why politicians and advertisers cultivate the art of creating an image that is able to convince voters or consumers. Isn't it said that a picture is worth a thousand words? For children and adolescents, images speak, encapsulate, and then recall the essence of new information. The more immediately applicable the image is to a problem that the child has to solve, the more likely it is that his new awareness of the meaning of the image will be profound, and the easier it will be for him to change his attitude.

For example, when dealing with a problem of stress that the young person puts on himself, either through his own counterproductive behavior, negative obsessive thoughts, an unhealthy perfectionism, or through the fear of judgment of others, I suggest you use an elastic band and guide him through the following activity. Ask the student to hold the elastic band so that there is no tension on it and then to show you, by stretching the elastic band, the level of internal tension he feels when he engages in certain behaviors. For each item that you mention, or that you ask him to state, the student should apply and maintain a certain level of tension on the elastic band until he physically feels the effect—in his arm muscles—of the continuous stress to which he is subjecting himself. You can begin the exercise with, for example, the tension level that results from using disrespectful language with the teacher or with school administrators. This initial tension is immediately redoubled, because such behavior automatically has consequences—revocation of privileges, breakdown of cooperation, loss of trust, threats of punishment etc.—all of which increase the student's stress level even more, whether he is conscious of it or not. Next, have him boost the degree of internal tension even higher by invoking his indifferent and careless attitude toward his schoolwork or his exams: what effect does the possibility of a test or a presentation have on the elastic band?

The first part of this experiment ends when the elastic band is stretched to its maximum degree, the second part then reverses the process, as you ask the student to relax the tension in proportion to the constructive attitudes that lessen his inner tension. For example, if he hands in his work on time and is proud of the result, or if he spontaneously and willingly contributes to a group activity, how will these attitudes affect the tension of the elastic band and, by analogy, his internal stress? It is particularly important that the student experiences the benefits of relaxing the tension in his body and that he is able to physically contrast the slackening with the tensing. Don't forget to leave the elastic band with him, so it will act as a reminder and enable him to continue to think about this issue.

4   Making abstractions concrete

The use of images or objects that are part of what the student already knows well to represent a problem or behavior, offers the benefit of making more abstract concepts immediately concrete—like the internal stress shown by the elastic band. The cerebral maturity required for the comprehension of abstract ideas often exceeds the intellectual competencies of children—and even of teenagers—for whom it can be difficult to fully understand what, for example, "shyness" might be. Rather than coming out with grand adult principles and attempting to fervently explain to the student the importance of asserting himself and taking his rightful place in life, here's an exercise that can be much more effective, because it is more concrete and therefore better adapted to the level of development of your young students.

On a blank sheet of paper, faintly sketch out a drawing that the child is unable to recognize due to its paleness. Then gradually retrace the drawing so as to make it more and more clear, so the student can recognize it. Now make a parallel between your first sketch and a shy, self-effacing person, who no one notices because he doesn't put himself forward and does-n't clearly express what he wants to say. Finally, make a comparison between the last pic-ture and someone who speaks sufficiently loudly and clearly, who articulates well and uses correct language. If necessary, you can take the comparison further, by drawing a line that is so hard that the tip of the pencil tears the paper. In this way you will illustrate that a person who is too assertive or too domineering can sometimes harm the quality of relationships with others. For each level of self-assertiveness, the child will from now on possess an image. He can define and consider himself as too pale or too dark, or acknowledge the paleness of oth-ers. In short, he will now be able to play with the concept and refine it according to his sub-sequent observations.

Another way to make shyness more evident in the eyes of the child is to ask him to shake a dice, without ever rolling it. While the child is doing this, the teacher begins to make a paral-lel between the perpetually irresolute gesture and the fact that the child himself often hesi-tates to make decisions or to dare to express himself within the group, while thinking at length about the consequences of his involvement in class, of the best way to get involved, and so on, without ever managing to take the first steps, to move to action, or to take his place. Help him realize that when the dice isn't rolled, no result can be achieved (0), yet as soon as the dice hits the table, you have the opportunity of getting at least a 1 and maybe even a 6! In the same way, the mere fact of daring and moving forward will necessarily pro-duce a more valuable experience than remaining immobile and uncertain, nurturing his fear of the judgment of others.

5 Short lessons are more easily remembered than long ones

Educators often forget this fundamental principle: several short items of information are more easily remembered than a lengthy speech. Bear in mind, when you wish to improve a par-ticular aspect of a student's or the group's behavior, that you should target a little bit at a time, especially with elementary school children. You should divide the task into small activities and clearly formulate your instructions in small units so they are easy to take in.

To encourage the success of one of the more difficult activities to coordinate in class—namely, working in teams—you can take time to explain the series of stages to reach by giv-ing each one a specific movement. For example, you determine with the students what the signal will be for the end of small group discussions: you raise your hand, which signifies that the current exercise is now over. When the students realize that you have raised your hand, they must hurry to do the same in turn. Due to the snowball effect, even if one of them is not looking at you, he will see his neighbor's raised hand and will immediately understand the message. You can also use intermediary signals to manage the various stages of a workshop project: for example, if you raise only one finger, you are indicating that the first part of the exercise is over, or that the first scheduled activity has just ended; by raising two fingers, you are signaling that it is time for the second part to start etc. In this way, you can complete ten steps without having to say a single word or to repeat new instructions over and over again to ensure that the students have all fully understood.

6 The whole is more easily remembered than an isolated element

When you want to retain a sequence of varied information, there are two ways to proceed: if I gave you a series of ten words like *rose, cloud, printer, bird, bread, fireplace, bed, plank, heart,* and *book*, you could attempt to keep them in that order. After several tedious repetitions, you would probably succeed, but you would get there more easily and far quicker if you created links uniting each of the disparate elements. Thus, to give a logical association to these objects, you could invent a story.

A giant *rose*, the same size, color and texture as a *cloud* had been placed next to a giant *printer*, which, having never smelled anything so sweet, was touched to the point of pouring out its feelings. It confessed that it had let the pages it was printing fly away like *bird*s, until they touched the ground where upon they became real birds. In complete happiness, they gleaned here and there little scraps of dry *bread*, which they found in a carefully maintained *fireplace* in a magnificent park, probably left there by regular visitors. Also, in an enchanted corner of the park, a *bed* made of old worm-eaten *plank*s had been prepared, arranged in the shape of a *heart* and on which a *book* was delicately placed.

Now would you be able to repeat the order of the 10 words in the list without looking at the text? This mnemonic method dates back at least to the time of the Romans: Cicero used this technique to retain the major arguments of his legal discourse. For example, he would mentally distribute, in each room of his house, a symbol that summarized an argument he wished to present. He would then "walk through" his house in his mind as he proceeded to give his oral arguments, "picking up" the reminders of each point he wanted to mention as he went. In the context of classroom management, reinforcing the memorization of instructions by building a metaphor with an object will let the object alone *become* the instructions for the students. The use of such a metaphor/signal, for example, expresses directly the rule to be followed, while recalling to memory the entire discussion it symbolizes.

Let's take the traffic-light technique, which is also used for the management of talking in class and that keeps the number of repetitions by the teacher to a minimum (of the "That's enough. The exercise is finished. Quiet please ..." kind). By commenting on a representation of traffic lights with the students, ensure that they fully understand the risks related to not respecting signals. By not moving when the light is green, we obstruct the traffic and the other drivers become impatient, honk their horns, and may even try to go around us—thus risking a collision. When the light is yellow, if we accelerate rather than brake, we're very likely to cause an accident. By running a red light, we further increase the likelihood of causing an accident or injury, and also of receiving a ticket, which would punish our thoughtless recklessness. After this discussion with the group, give each light a specific value: the red light imposes silence; the green gives freedom to discuss, exchange ideas or work in groups; the yellow light indicates a need to slow down and reduce discussion as the exercise is about to finish and they will soon need to be quiet. The teacher, who can then move between the rows displaying the yellow light, and then the red, will save her voice and energy. The teacher is able to direct the activities in a much less irritating way for both herself and her students, who generally appreciate the originality of the method and conform easily to the instructions conveyed in this way.

This technique can also help to develop better interpersonal relationships: the red light indicates to a chatty and exuberant student that it would be a good idea to quiet down and leave room for others to express their opinions. The yellow light acts as a signal representing the need to think about the relevance of a comment before expressing it, while the green light gives a push in the right direction to the shyer class members, to start the first exchange with another.

7 Speak to the whole brain

The more a message addresses the whole of the brain, the more deeply and efficiently it will be recorded: a multisensory approach, which solicits not only language but also sight and other forms of concrete experience, favors a better integration of concepts. The information is imprinted in different cerebral zones, which constitute many possible reference points for the recollection of the information.

For example, you are struggling with a student who is being sufficiently unruly to disturb the class, but not yet troublesome enough to warrant suspension. You have spoken with him on numerous occasions, but nothing has changed; he continues his little games, convinced that what he is doing has no consequences, and will have none in the future. To help him become aware of the immediate and long-term consequences of his attitude, during a one-on-one session have the disruptive student stand in front of your desk, facing you, and ask him to take a step backward or sideways (depending upon where the classroom door is located) each time that you mention an action he has taken that disturbed the entire class. For example: "When I asked you to stop talking to your neighbor, you kept on doing it, so take a step back (toward the door)." He will implicitly feel that he is distancing himself from you while getting closer to the door. In the process, he'll realize that his behavior cannot be tolerated indefinitely and that it has unquestionably created a distance between himself and you, and brought him closer to getting a suspension. If necessary, lead him physically, step by step, out to the corridor, and leave him there a few seconds so that he can completely grasp what the ultimate outcome of his current attitude will be. Next, you can do something that will be very beneficial to him in the future: make him take a few steps toward you as you mention what actions he can take to improve his behavior. By experiencing the effects of both forms of behavior in this way, he will be all the more motivated to replace his former habits with new ways of behaving.

Because this exercise addresses the implicit memory of the student via his body, it will not be necessary for you to lecture on the negative or positive consequences of the attitude that he intends to develop from now on—he knows. Moreover, each of the precise movements and actions that he has effectively made constitutes another anchor, which registers the information in several regions of the brain. It is somewhat like having several keys to your front door that you've hidden in different places: you're almost guaranteed that you'll always be able to get in because, if you forget where one key is, there is always another one available somewhere!

8 An allergy to criticism

It's an undeniable fact: negative criticism paralyzes students' memories. Reprimands and accusations render inoperative the neuronal circuits that record and recall information. Nothing the teacher says registers, and even things already learned aren't remembered. For example, you give in to the surge of exasperation that has suddenly invaded you when you notice that Lawrence isn't working and is *still* dawdling! "You still haven't started the exercise? And after all the discussion we've had about the new resolutions that you made! How can you expect me to trust you?" In all likelihood the tension will increase or Lawrence will close himself up even more than before: you will have lost the contact. Instead, if you ask him simply: "You're not thirsty today?" Lawrence will perhaps grumble about being brought back to order, but there's a good chance that he will start working. By simply evoking the idea of thirst, you do not denigrate Lawrence, you don't devalue him, and you don't damage your relationship.

Instead, what you've accomplished is to jog his memory back to the discussion that you had, during which you presented him with a glass of water and asked him how thirsty he was (a little, a lot, or not at all). The first time, you had pointed out the relationship between the degree of thirst and how much he will drink: the thirstier he is, the more he will want to drink, the less thirsty he is, the less he will feel the need to drink. You then created a parallel with the interest that he brings to class and the quality of his learning. The less thirst for learning that he has, the less he will take in the information and the less efficiently he will integrate it. On the other hand, the thirstier he is to learn, the greater his desire to access new knowledge and deepen the knowledge he acquires. From then on, Lawrence just needs to hear a reference to this discussion ("Are you thirsty today?") to immediately arouse more concentrated attention. The allusion to the metaphor remains relatively neutral and allows you to encourage the thirst for knowledge in a positive way, by emphasizing the solution and not the problem.

Nothing can replace repetition

Repetitions remain, in good educational methods, necessary and indispensable: they reinforce and consolidate learning. What you can always reduce are long speeches, which become as tiresome for the speaker as for the audience. You need to find effective reminders for your instructions that enable you to reactivate a message without having to say it. Images, objects, and signs possess the valuable advantage of immediately recalling to the student's memory all the meaning you have attached to them. In this way, you can repeat and reiterate the same message by different means: by making a brief allusion to an image, by pointing directly to an illustration or an object, or even by making a gesture whose meaning you and the student have agreed upon. Thus, you reinforce the memory circuits that contain the information to be mastered.

Furthermore, there are instructions that a teacher needs to constantly repeat, for the simple reason that his task is to help the children to acquire personal, interpersonal and intellectual competencies that will serve them for their entire lives. However, let's take discipline as an example. We can agree with what Scott Peck wrote in his book, *The Road Less Traveled*,[3] that it is not just one of the most useful strengths to impart to a child, but also one of the most difficult to master. Very few adults exceed 6/10 in this regard. If we take the example of the discipline required to do physical exercise, we see that despite all the knowledge of the benefits of physical activity, the majority of people always find excuses when it comes to actually doing it … and especially to keeping at it on a regular basis. Consequently, do you think it is realistic to expect this from a child or teenager? By holding reasonable expectations for your students, you avoid being disappointed by their breaches of discipline and can continue to repeat the same instructions without feeling irritated.

Here is an illustration* that translates this principle well:

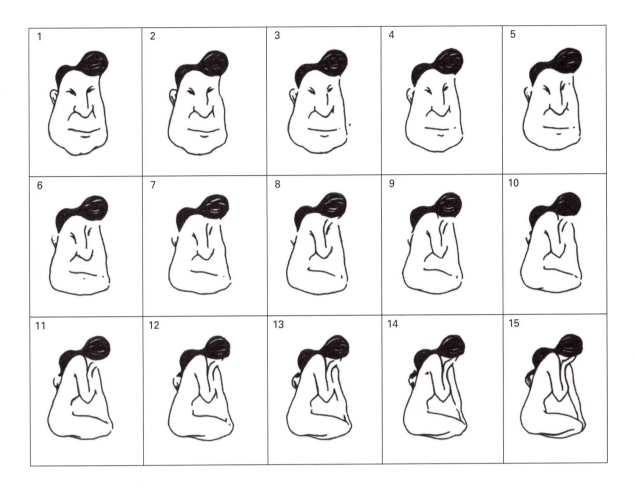

What do you see in the first picture? A man's face, isn't it? And in the last one, what can you make out? One or two women? Now, can you spot the changes that have been made between figures 3 and 4? Or between 12 and 13? Difficult, isn't it? As educators, we sometimes expect a student to go from the first condition to the fifteenth in a single bound; this is excessive and discouraging. Changes are made slowly and gradually, in humans as in other species. If you know how to recognize and support each of the little steps in the right direction, the young person will progressively improve his behavior. Sometimes, you have to look long and hard to find the little details that have changed from one picture to another; the same goes for the behavior of students. It is vital to find and clearly identify these improvements so that progress can continue; acknowledgment of this evolution, however hesitant it may be, acts as the motor for change. Without it, the progress stops.

* Illustration taken from my book
Techniques d'Impact pour Grandir destinées aux adolescents, p. 84.

10 ... because what is encouraged persists and develops;
what is discouraged shrinks and disappears

The law of reinforcement is a natural phenomenon and student behavior is no exception to it. If you vary the reminder signals of an instruction, you directly encourage the student to follow that instruction; then, if you warmly underscore the completion of the task, it will be done even better the next time. On the other hand, when criticisms are the only thing expressed, it erodes the desire to do well: the student begins to think that he will never succeed in satisfying you and will decide not to bother—before even beginning his work. Thus, the smallest action that leads in the direction of the learning you are instilling in him must be noted, duly highlighted and congratulated—make it up if you need to! Because it is on the basis of these little affirmations that a new behavior pattern can root itself and grow.

11 We only remember 20% of what we are told

If I have particularly insisted, throughout this book, on the role and importance of implicit memory in *Impact Techniques in the Classroom*, it is because the explicit memory that is generally used exclusively in formal education—which is based on language, logic, and rationality—only holds 20% of all learning, according to the American researcher Bessel Van der Kolk.[4] On the other hand, the implicit memory—which is transmitted through the senses and sensations—is responsible for 80% of what we retain. One of the main impacts of this phenomenon is that a perfect adjustment between what you say and your attitude, posture, facial expression, and tone of voice promotes better retention of your message in the mind of the student or group. That's why one needs to be "really there", whether you are talking to an individual student or to the whole class. If your mind is elsewhere, your body muddles the verbal message; furthermore, the incoherence between the words and the attitude will puzzle the student who will not know which message he is to pick up. A little girl says to her mother, "You're angry." The mother, with a frown and a scowl, responds, "No, I'm not angry!" The little girl says, "Yes, you really are angry." To which the mother answers, "I said I wasn't!" and the child concludes, "Then tell that to your face!" Do you think that the child believed what her mother was saying or did she believe what she felt and saw? The implicit memory is always the one that prevails, showing the importance of paying particular attention to our actions, expressions, and tone of voice.

12 Memory is much more emotional than one would think

It is largely by virtue of the principle of emotional investment that enthusiastic teachers easily transmit "living" knowledge that will in turn fascinate their students. The significant teachers who punctuate your own academic journey like so many glittering jewels are generally those who knew how to give you special attention, however brief. With that teacher, you felt understood and had the impression that you really counted. These teachers knew how to exert a real influence on your life, and if you ponder it for while, you will still be able to remember what you learned from them because they knew how to reach your heart. Daniel Goleman highlights, in *Emotional Intelligence*,[5] that an event that is accompanied by an emotion is imprinted more directly and more deeply in the circuits of the brain. By using Impact Techniques—which call on play, laughter, and surprise, but most importantly are accompanied by extra investment on your part—you periodically give your student or your class a superior type of attention to that of your normal teaching. It will therefore be possible to foster in them "happy memories" while liberating you from the exhausting role of the broken record, worn out through too much use!

----

[1] M.S. Gazzaniga, "The Split Brain Revisited", 1999, p. 130.

[2] B. Van der Kolk, A. McFarlane, and L. Weisaeth, 1996.

[3] S. Peck, 1978.

[4] B. Van der Kolk, A. McFarlane, and L. Weisaeth, 1996.

[5] *Emotional Intelligence I*, 1997.

Impact Techniques
using OBJECTS

This section suggests some simple methods using objects that you would find in your environment to deal with various difficulties that may be encountered in the classroom or with some students. Their accessibility and simplicity make these the tools of choice for the effective communication of knowledge to your students.

Impact techniques using OBJECTS

1

THE WORRY JAR

PURPOSE Distractions, worries and concerns not only interfere with concentration in the classroom but they also create other problems, by spoiling the understanding of a lesson, by causing poorer results, and eventually by causing students to fall behind, which must then be caught up on.

YOU WILL NEED

A glass jar, with a label that reads, "Distractions, Worries, and Concerns".

● INDIVIDUAL ●●● CLASS

The teacher informs the student or students that this jar is especially reserved for worries or concerns they may have about their family, health, financial resources of the family (or those at their disposal), what other people think about their clothes etc. The jar can also contain all kinds of distractions: fleeting thoughts about the next vacation, weekend or evening activities, their favorite TV program, recreation, an upcoming oral presentation etc. Before beginning the class, the teacher reminds the students that anyone who needs to should put any thoughts that might undermine their concentration in the jar and then close it tightly (so that no troublesome thoughts can get out). The jar will remain closed until the end of the day, when the students may reappropriate their worries and distractions if they wish. In the meantime, the students won't have been disturbed by these thoughts and will have been able to give their full efforts by remaining attentive to the lessons that were given to them. If it happens that a student nevertheless succumbs to distraction, the teacher can simply show him the jar while reinforcing the reminder with a little tap on the shoulder. The explanation given at the start of the day should swiftly be recalled, which saves time, energy, and, furthermore, reinforces the feeling of collaboration between the student and teacher and even among all the students in the class. In this same spirit of collaboration, the teacher could also request the privilege of the worry jar, by informing the students, for example, that not much space remains in the container because so many things have been put in it. By confiding to the class that he also needs to set aside certain worries, the adult reinforces the student's self-discipline over his thoughts.

2

THE $20 DOLLAR BILL

PURPOSE However much attention the teaching staff give to the problems of rejection in class, it remains difficult to put an end to the collective cruelty inflicted on a student who is unanimously designated the scapegoat of the group and who is constantly ridiculed and ostracized.

YOU WILL NEED

A $20 dollar bill (or a smaller bill if the student is younger).

INDIVIDUAL The teacher shows the bill to the student who is the victim of rejection, asking him what its value is. After the student answers, the teacher then crumples up the bill with an energy similar to that used by the child's "aggressors", with spite and perhaps even a certain degree of delight—stomping on the bill and crushing it, using as much as possible the destructive remarks and gibes that are usually thrown at the child. The teacher ensures that the student identifies with the bill by asking, for example: "This is what they do to you, isn't it? Do you feel a bit like this? Do you feel rejected, crushed by everyone and not worth very much? Do you think that the others are right to treat you like that? Do you also think that you aren't worth very much?" When the student replies affirmatively, the teacher picks up the bill with more respect, straightens it out carefully, and asks again, "How much is this bill worth?" The student recognizes that the value of the bill is still the same, identical to what it was at the beginning, no matter how it was treated. You can make him understand that, similarly, in spite of what the others say to him and the way in which they treat him, his value stays intact and unchanged. This image generally proves to be fairly strong and graphic so that the student takes on a new confidence and is capable of maintaining his self-confidence by showing a certain detachment when the others try to destabilize him or reject him.

A variation of this technique can prove to be even more effective with younger children. On a sheet of paper, the student herself writes down the qualities that characterize her (intelligent, kind, warm, honest etc.). The teacher goes through the same demonstration as described above, but with the student's sheet of paper. After having smoothed out the crumpled paper, the teacher asks if the qualities are still written on the paper; obviously, they haven't disappeared. The child can keep the paper as a reminder and to anchor the benefits of the discussion more deeply.

3

TRAFFIC LIGHTS

PURPOSE

This technique is intended to enable better management of talking in the classroom by limiting the teacher's interventions—and so limiting the irritation of having to repeat the same message over and over again ("That's enough. The exercise is finished. Quiet please."). By simply moving between the rows, showing a yellow light and then a red one, the teacher saves his voice and energy in a much less irritating way, both for her and for the students, who will generally appreciate the originality of this method and comply more easily with instructions given this way.

YOU WILL NEED

An image of traffic lights (green, red, and yellow).

CLASS

Make sure that the students fully understand the risks involved in not respecting traffic lights; by not moving when the light is green, the traffic is obstructed, drivers in other cars become impatient, honk their horns, and may even try to drive around—thus risking a collision. When the light is yellow, if you were to accelerate rather than brake, you'd be very likely to cause an accident. By running a red light, you further increase the likelihood of causing an accident or injury, and also of receiving a ticket, which would punish your thoughtless recklessness. After this discussion with the group, give each light a specific value: the red light imposes silence; the green light gives full freedom to discuss, exchange ideas, or work in teams; the yellow light indicates a need to slow down and reduce discussion as the exercise is about to finish and they will soon need to be quiet again.

INDIVIDUAL This technique may help a shyer student to take the first steps when he needs to, when he should take part in class or interact with the others. By giving him multiple images of a green light (and only a green light), that he can keep with him, you give him multiple "opportunities" to use the symbol. The images are like many little pushes that will help him, each time, to initiate contact with another, so as to little by little overcome his shyness. Encourage the student to think of each use of a green light as a try, an attempt, or a game and never as an obligation. The curiosity of seeing what will happen if he takes the first steps should prevail over the fear of being rejected. If the opening that he offers to another is refused, it's not a serious problem; it may just mean that the other person wasn't the right person to interact with at that moment.

INDIVIDUAL In addition, the images of the yellow and red lights will help remind a young chatterbox that before speaking and interrupting or dominating the conversation, she should be sure that she respects the rules of interpersonal communication. The yellow light will help her to question the pertinence and value of what she has to say and bring to her attention the fact that someone else may be speaking or about to speak. As for the red light, this represents either a subject about which she should not speak (a secret, or a delicate or painful subject for someone else in the group), or a period of silence that must be complied with.

4

HIDDEN CONTENTS

PURPOSE   This technique enables you to commence a discussion with a concerned and worried student who seems to be battling with a serious problem.

YOU WILL NEED

An opaque container and its lid (jar, coffee cup etc.), filled with paper clips, keys, coins, chalk, various objects that make a sound when shaken but that are difficult to identify when you cannot see them.

INDIVIDUAL

While moving the container so as all the hidden items make a noise, ask the student if he knows what is hidden inside. Ensure that you have inserted enough different objects so that his responses can't mention all the items inside the container, so that the exercise continues to the point when the fact that he isn't able to discover what is hidden causes a kind of discomfort. You can then explain to him that he is like the container with the secret contents; he is also hiding something within himself, in his heart. Just as it is impossible for him to know what is concealed in the container, you cannot guess or see what is inside him. Explain that the only way to free himself of the burden that is weighing him down is to open the lid and express what is bothering him. Even if the student does not confide immediately after this discussion (which most often proves to be the case with teenagers), he will be touched by your offer and support, and will feel understood straight away, even before explaining what is worrying him. If he continues to keep quiet, you can nevertheless mention that you are always there and show him the container, saying, on the more difficult days, "I get the feeling that there are some more things that have been added today ..." or on better days, "It would seem that your jar has been lightened since we spoke last ..." The use of this technique reinforces without fail the confidence that the student has in you and, even if he is unable to confide his secret to you, your support and understanding are extremely beneficial to him.

5

OPENING HOURS

A number of different problems can be approached using this technique, such as concentration and attention, self-discipline in schoolwork, or even class dynamics.

YOU WILL NEED

A small sign such as those used by shop owners to indicate to their customers that the store is open or closed, as well as the hours.

INDIVIDUAL

Ask a student when he arrives in class if he is "open" or "closed" to being taught that day. If he stays closed, either due to serious concerns, more trivial distractions, or because his extremely negative attitude toward school or the teacher determines all of his behavior, you can remind him to open his intellectual store by changing the sign and voluntarily opening himself up to his studies. With the rebellious teenager, with whom you have tried many approaches, you could make him understand as a last resort that it is useless to come to class if he remains irreparably "closed".

INDIVIDUAL

This technique also allows for discussion with the student about his management of study and homework: when he gets home, is he "open" or "closed" to his school work? In the evening? And on Saturday mornings? Has he chosen his own opening hours for schoolwork? What are the most productive times that would allow him to work well outside school?

●●● CLASS The relationships between students determine and influence the productivity of each of the members of the group. Discuss with them how open or closed their general attitude is with regard to others in the class; are they open to listening to and welcoming the comments and questions of others? From everyone, even those who are ostracized? This reflection on receptive and attentive attitudes can be followed up with a question about the consequences of opening up to others. Be sure that the students identify, among the benefits of openness, a significant complicity between all the members of the group, the general feeling of confidence that a student will have when she knows she can express herself without being criticized, and the sense of responsibility that a student will feel when he knows to withhold damaging comments.

The discussion should also emphasize, that, in contrast, a closed attitude necessarily implies aggressiveness, tension, distance, coldness, and lack of productivity. Lead each student to realize that he is personally responsible for the open or closed sign shown in class; does he assume this responsibility truly and completely? Does he leave the decision of his own openness to others, by adopting the stance taken by one of the leaders in the class? How would the students react if they had to walk in front of every one of their classmates showing the appropriate side of their open/closed signs to define their relationships with the others in the class?

6

VIDEO CASSETTE

PURPOSE This technique will enable you, from the very beginning of the session, to manage the classroom in a way that is motivating for both the students and the teacher, by presenting the year to come as a collective project.

YOU WILL NEED

A selection of video cassettes, of which some are new and still in their packaging.

●●● CLASS At the beginning of the school year, the teacher shows the group a blank cassette, indicating that it will represent their school year, from September to June. Each of the members of the class, including the teacher, is an actor in this film, but also director, scriptwriter, producer, cameraman etc. It is therefore up to each person to decide if the film will be interesting or boring and unpleasant. What will be the criteria for a successful class film? The students may identify concentration; respect for instructions; mutual aid and support brought to those who come up against more difficulties than others; the self-discipline of each student to do their homework and study; civility and kindness; honesty etc. (The teacher will adapt the criteria for success according to the age of the group and her personal objectives.) The presentation of this cassette to be realized together should end on a positive note, as the teacher assures her students that she has complete confidence in them and that she is certain that her film will be the best of her career, because before her are excellent, well-motivated, and very talented actors.

●●● CLASS To obtain even more convincing results, the discussion can continue further, this time using cassettes from the past: the teacher therefore presents to the group pre-recorded cassettes, saying that they are from previous school years, and asks each student to describe what he is most proud of and then to express what he was most hurt and disturbed by. The act of identifying types of hurtful or destructive behavior in front of the others helps to avoid the repetition of such behavior during the forthcoming year: knowing what has already aggrieved one of them, the group will avoid reproducing the same actions or attitudes. Furthermore, elements of pride will be integrated into the program for the coming year, because each person will want to repeat as often as possible those actions that have given him significant satisfaction in the past. Don't forget to leave the cassettes in a visible place within the classroom so as to firmly anchor the symbol and what it represents, and to stimulate the students to keep it in mind throughout the year.

●●● CLASS

The teacher can also write the title on the cassette (for example, Mrs Butler's Class, 2004–2005) and use it again at the end of the year to evaluate their journey.

7

Paper clips

YOU WILL NEED

Paper clips, to attach paper together.

●●● CLASS The teacher asks the students to attach some sheets of paper together using a paper clip (or does it him- or herself), pointing out the use of this type of clip enables them to join different parts of the same document securely. The clip can be tested concretely by the teacher, by trying to pull out one page of the bundle held by the clip. The students will gain from this demonstration the image of an indissociable whole. Then, the teacher leads the members of the class to question their propensity to attach their concentration, attention, interest, and enjoyment to each piece of work. By attaching all these elements to one project, the student gives himself a very good chance of obtaining the best result possible. Ask them to think about the times when they have effectively connected these elements of success, and then to remember their feelings of personal satisfaction when the work was returned or when the corrected copies were received. During the next exercise in class, clearly show a paper clip to the entire class to encourage each student to revise her method and to give her best to the task at hand. In so doing, you can refresh the memory of the group without having to repeat the instructions symbolized by the paper clip.

8

SUGGESTION BOX

PURPOSE

The box can be used by students in many different situations. The comments deposited in the box can be anonymous and include suggestions that would improve the class dynamic or the effectiveness of lessons. The box can also be used for confidences too weighty for a child or adolescent who can't clearly express what is disturbing him (worries at home, concerns in class), or for those secret confidences that someone else has confided to a child who now doesn't know what to do (the unplanned pregnancy of a friend).

YOU WILL NEED

An attractive box, made by the teacher or specially bought, to receive the suggestions or confidences of the students.

●●● CLASS

In explaining the function of this box and by making it available to the class, the teacher makes sure that each student feels more involved in the group. The teacher acknowledges the importance and value of each of his students: their opinions and comments will be read, taken into consideration and, as far as possible and according to the circumstances, will be implemented or shared with the group. The request for help, coming from a teacher who is open to the suggestions of his students, usually generates a lot of creativity among many young people. This technique proves to be very worthwhile, insofar as it makes everyone aware of the life of the group and its objectives by favoring the expression of all ideas.

●●● CLASS

In the case of anonymous confidences, it is not necessarily important that you succeed in tracing the author of the note. It is more than enough, in this context, for the student to know that the note will be read. The feeling of liberation that follows a confession and the support that you offer constitute the first steps toward an open, face-to-face discussion.

9

MIXING SUBSTANCES

PURPOSE **This technique aims to illustrate in concrete terms the phenomena of contamination to those students who are often too easily influenced by others.**

YOU WILL NEED

Liquids that react together, like coffee and milk, juice and water, or orange juice and milk, depending on the objective of the demonstration.

INDIVIDUAL Depending on the case, the teacher will draw a parallel between the reaction of certain substances to each other and a relationship to be preserved, improved, or abandoned. The relationship in question may be with a friend to whom it would be worth apologizing and making up for a mistake; with another student to whom he should stand up for himself more strongly; or with an acquaintance from whom it would be preferable to distance himself. Adapt the choice of liquids to each situation. When coffee and milk are mixed, the two liquids change color, to create a new color that merges both perfectly: this mixture could symbolize a complementary relationship where each brings something to the other in a way that suits both. When you pour grape juice, orange juice, or apple juice into a container with water, the juice maintains its color and assimilates the water (there is no longer any clear or transparent liquid): here you obtain a representation of an unequal relationship between one person who makes no compromises and keeps his position constantly and a second person who is self-effacing and submits to the first. As for the reaction that occurs between orange or lemon juice and milk, this illustrates a mixture of incompatible elements, because the milk curdles immediately.

INDIVIDUAL This technique also lets you initiate a discussion of the relationship of a student with her family, with other teachers, or with even you. Ask her to mix the substances in a way in which the result illustrates what she thinks of the relationship in question: in this way you will obtain clear and more explicit information than she would have perhaps said in words. It may well be easier for her to translate her thoughts through this image of, for

example, a "curdled milk"-type relationship, and then to describe what makes her uncomfortable in it.

INDIVIDUAL

Beyond interpersonal relationships, the mixing of substances can also be used to comment on the behavior of the child in school. By mixing studies and drugs, you end up, without fail, with milk curdled by lemon juice. Distractions dilute study efforts, like in the mixture of water and juice, and may cause interest in school to completely disappear. Perseverance, attention, and constructive thoughts, on the other hand, combine with school to yield a complementary mixture that increases interest and satisfaction with regard to progress in class and good results.

TIP

Simple rewards

This technique is designed to improve the students' attitude toward work while maximizing the value of the reward that they will eventually receive.

People who don't plan their vacations until a week before benefit much less than those who have given thought to their trip and anticipated the various stops on their itinerary several months in advance. For the latter, the benefits are not restricted to one week of vacation only, but accumulate during all the preceding months when they imagine their vacation. In class you can use a similar technique, especially when you approach a more arduous and difficult section of material. First, announce to the group that there will be a nice pause for replenishment after the next work period: the students will be more enthusiastic, have better concentration and be well disposed to cooperate, as they already know that they will earn a reward for their efforts. This will count on two fronts, as it will have been hoped for before being enjoyed.

10

Stop, Pause, and Go

PURPOSE **This technique is similar to that of Traffic Lights (n° 3), but has a stronger evocative value—and thus will prove more effective— among students who have difficulties in mobilizing their energy and attention at the right moment.**

YOU WILL NEED
A representation of the "stop", "pause", and "play" buttons from a remote control, or three posterboards, with different colored images of a starter's flag (used to signal "go" for a race), a stop sign, and a pause signal (like that on a remote control).

INDIVIDUAL To use this technique for work on interpersonal relationships, with shy or, at the other extreme, overexuberant students, consult the traffic lights technique (n° 3), from which you will easily be able to transfer the principal elements.

●●● CLASS The "go" flag gives the start signals in all kinds of competition events; the students are well aware of its meaning and usually react very well to its presentation, understanding that they must start their work without delay. The "stop" sign also carries strong connotations and is familiar to all; it causes a more immediate effect than a verbal instruction indicating the end of an activity or the cessation of distractions. The "pause" symbol, for its part, attracts the students' attention to advice and recommendations prior to an exercise or an exam. These symbols prove particularly well adapted for school activities that generate anxiety and tension in students, like exams and oral presentations. In these situations, the use of signs rather than verbal commands mobilizes students' potential more quickly. They're able to control their attention and concentration more easily, thus avoiding letting nerves and anxiety dilute their efforts.

11

EXTENSION CORD

YOU WILL NEED

An extension cord.

INDIVIDUAL The teacher first discusses with the student the utility of an extension cord, which allows a machine to be plugged in and supplied with electricity, even if it is a fair distance from an electrical outlet. Then make the parallel between this situation and that of the student you are talking to, who doesn't understand new information as well as the others, because he is distant from—or has distanced himself from—the electrical outlets and cannot connect to them directly. Stress that the distance from the point does not ever put into question the potential quality and performance of the machine; it is simply necessary to use an extension cord to enable him to be plugged in and able to function at full capacity. The "extension cord" may mean receiving help from a special-education teacher, a therapist, or a tutor.

Evidently, if the plug is not plugged in, the machine cannot function, even if an extension cord is provided. To be able to plug himself in at the right place, the child or teenager must use the appropriate extension cord, which fits the correct electric outlet. Consequently, the extension cord made up of a circle of poorly adjusted friends or a problematic peer group may interfere with an effective connection to school. By exercising a bad influence and reinforcing harmful behaviors, these types of "support systems", far from supplying energy, can actually involve high costs in the long run, such as the consumption of drugs or alcohol, delinquency, or other unproductive behaviors. Examine with the student the types of extension cords that are available to him and analyze whether they connect him to sources that truly supply him with energizing power and help him to explore and exploit all his potential.

12

Battery

┌─────────┐
│ PURPOSE │
└─────────┘
This object will represent the necessity to give oneself time to stop in order to recharge and regain full energy levels.

YOU WILL NEED

One rechargeable battery.

┌─────────────┐
│ ● INDIVIDUAL │
└─────────────┘
To make the application of the battery even more concrete, the teacher can question the student as follows: What do we usually use this type of battery for? For what kind of machine do we use them? Where do you get them from? What happens when the battery is exhausted? Just like rechargeable batteries, we all need to recharge our energy levels when we have done too much work, or put a lot of effort or energy into certain aspects of our lives. With younger children, recharge occurs when they sleep: with a child that is reluctant to go to sleep, take the time to explain that a good night's sleep re-establishes strength and makes all his energy available again for the next day. With older children, depending on the case, recharging can be translated in various ways. Investing more energy in his work beforehand, and consequently getting a greater feeling of self-worth from the results, is the best way to get a boost of energy for the child who habitually gets little satisfaction from school. On the other hand, for the child who is rather compulsive with regard to his scholarly performances, it would be more a question of setting time aside for enjoying himself with his friends, or perhaps giving a little more attention to his appearance or diet, starting friendships or nurturing romances, or setting aside extra time for sleep. Make sure that he knows how to identify the times when his battery is running low and whether he knows some ways to recharge it effectively.

┌─────────────┐
│ ●●● CLASS   │
└─────────────┘
The battery enables you to introduce an activity enjoyed by the whole group and to make it more effective, allowing everyone to recharge. Using the symbol of the battery, the students will understand that even in the context of school, it is important to reserve some quality time for activities that divert the mind away from the demands of the school program for a few moments, allowing the students to then return to their work with more focus and enthusiasm.

13

Mirror

PURPOSE This technique aims to reinforce attitudes of tolerance and understanding, by encouraging each student to recognize his own shortcomings and weaknesses.

YOU WILL NEED

A mirror, placed in the classroom for the whole year.

CLASS First, discuss the use of a mirror, which, by reflecting our image, allows us to evaluate our appearance and correct it where necessary. Then explain that the mirror will have a symbolic function in the class and will be used daily to remind each person that before criticizing a friend, a fellow student, or the teacher, it would be a good idea to take a look in the mirror (figuratively, if not physically). Doing so encourages the students to evaluate their own behavior, by asking if there is nothing they should reproach themselves for and by taking a critical look at the way they treat others.

Suggest the following exercise to the group, which will also have the effect of reinforcing cohesion. The students find a partner and, as if they were looking into a mirror at each other, note the similarities that they find with their partner, bringing out the points that they share, getting to know each other better and creating support and alliances between them. These similarities may be with respect to interests, values, talents, aspirations, friends, or any other aspect of their lives. The more similarities there are between two people, the closer they become, and the more available they become to each other. The teacher may favor, therefore, pairs made up of students who haven't yet been able to create real contact between them and thus consolidate links uniting the class members.

14

HEADPHONES

Depending on the system the headphones are connected to, the listener will hear what is being emitted from the system: it is not the headphones that diffuse the information.

YOU WILL NEED

Headphones of different types, like the ones inserted into the ear or the headset type that completely cover the outer ear.

CLASS The teacher presents to the group several types of headphone and asks those who wish to share with the others the experiences that they have had with this type of equipment. This part of the exercise is important, insofar as the more the memory of the experience is revived in the mind, the more receptive the students will be to the process of reflection that this exercise initiates. The teacher asks each student to question himself as to what kind of system he connects himself to when he is in class: to what the teacher is saying, to the activities of the night before or the next evening, to the discussions during recess, to the events of lunchtime. Is it the most profitable system? One that would help him achieve better results and greater satisfaction? What percentage of time is he tuned into listening during class? And to personal experiences and daydreaming? Evidently, a biological factor brought to light by Ernest Rossi must be taken into account (see Bibliography). He noticed that our diurnal and nocturnal cycles cause a brief moment of "switching-off" about every ninety minutes, during which our mind moves away from external preoccupation toward daydreaming—probably to recuperate physiologically. Consequently, it is necessary to ensure that periods of full attention in each cycle are maximized, devoting them especially to important activities (learning or work) and not squandering them on mental wanderings. The act of showing the headphones to the group allows you to remind them of this information without having to repeat it and will immediately reconnect the students to the contents of the lesson.

Microphone

PURPOSE This technique on self-assertion allows you to address the problems of young people who have difficulty "taking the mike" as well as those of students who can't put it down.

YOU WILL NEED

A microphone.

INDIVIDUAL To help a shy student evaluate his behavior and participation in class, ask him if he can manage to take the mike himself: if he isn't able to make himself do it, how can he be heard by the others? What are the consequences of this choice on his self-esteem? What effects does it have on how others treat him and how they regard him? Help the child or teenager to understand that when you do not give your opinion and show your presence, others end up forgetting you: nobody likes to be forgotten. Even if it is less confrontational to stay in the background in the short term, never overcoming embarrassment and shyness clearly and lastingly damages self-esteem in the long term.

CLASS Make an agreement with the group so that at least once a week, each will "take the mike" in class, but without exceeding a certain number of times (according to the number and type of students in the class). Mention to the group that each time a student offers a comment in class it will be noted, as far as possible, either by doing it yourself (but this task may seem a bit heavy), or by introducing a system whereby each student notes the contributions of a friend. In this case, the advantages of the technique are increased ten-fold by the fact that you are also introducing a synergistic class dynamic, where each student is linked to another and must ensure his role. This equality of responsibilities makes things easier for the more timid students and makes the more talkative ones more conscious of the disproportionate space they take up—all the more so since the requests of peers to speak or to be quiet are generally received better than those of the teacher.

16
PLUG

PURPOSE This technique is used to silence the more talkative members of the class in a way that spares the teacher's reserves of energy and patience. It can also be used to put an end to certain negative or destructive behavior patterns.

YOU WILL NEED

A bath, basin, or sink plug (preferably new!).

●●● CLASS You can present the plug whenever the loud, rowdy conduct of one or more student needs to be brought under control, or when continuous chatter interferes with the class. Many teachers, particularly at the high school level, hesitate to use this technique for fear that the teenagers in their class will react badly. However, those who have had the courage to use the plug have invariably obtained a better level of cooperation with the majority of their students—in general, a message delivered using a humorous symbol favors spontaneous cooperation.

● INDIVIDUAL To work with a student who picks on certain of his classmates, the teacher discusses the meaning of the plug so that the student develops the habit of interrupting his own denigrating remarks and stops fueling the cycle of rejection. The plug can also be used to help a student who has recently suffered a setback, by reminding her to put an end to the stream of negative and destructive thoughts that have overwhelmed her.

BRAKE AND ACCELERATOR

PURPOSE The use of these symbols makes the management of the class easier and allows the teacher to save energy.

YOU WILL NEED

Illustrations of the brake and accelerator pedals in a car.

●●● CLASS The teacher goes over the functions of the brake and accelerator pedals, explaining that the first slows down or stops the vehicle completely while the second initiates movement and increases speed. At the same time, emphasize that high speeds are more dangerous than moderate speeds; drivers need to obey the speed limits that help assure that they will arrive safe and sound at their destination without putting their safety at risk. The teacher will use the image of the accelerator to encourage some slower students not to dawdle along the way, to start work quickly when they need to do a given exercise or to make an effort to finish it before the time is up. The accelerator symbol helps you to motivate them to speed up without giving you that unpleasant feeling of pushing or scolding a student who is delaying everyone (the gesture is enough, there's no need to repeat it). With pre-school kids or even in the first few years of elementary school, the accelerator may be used when taking off or putting on coats, hats, and mittens, when getting started on a lesson, or when hurrying so as not to miss the bus. In high school, latecomers may be reminded with more humor using the image of the accelerator pedal rather than a sharp remark pointing out their late arrival in class. The image of the brake pedal, on the other hand, will reduce the speed—and increase the concentration—of students who tend to go too fast and consequently make lots of errors, who don't take the time to think before writing their answers or to re-read to check for spelling and accuracy. The teacher can develop the metaphor by explaining that going too fast increases the risk of accidents caused by lack of attention, which in turn have consequences on academic results. In addition, the brake can be used to moderate the class participation of students who know the material well and make it a source of pride to answer the teacher's questions first. Before posing a question to the group, the teacher can simply ask the overeager students concerned to apply the brakes and let the more shy or reserved members of the class formulate their responses.

18

X-RAY

This technique enables you to undertake a discussion with a student who you suspect has a problem, at home, at school, or in some other aspect of her life.

YOU WILL NEED

An X-ray, which you obtained from your doctor or medical clinic.

INDIVIDUAL

Show the student the X-ray, explaining that it is a photograph of the skeleton, which allows you to see inside the body to tell whether the bone structure is intact and in good health. Then, while speculating that it might be possible to do an X-ray of his heart, ask him what you would see: Are there any problems? Is there pain? Fear? Anger? If it were possible to do an X-ray of his family, would you see any particular problems? And if you took an X-ray of his feelings toward school, what would you find? In this way, you can explore different aspects of the child's life so as to find a trail that will indicate the nature of his problems—failing a clear response—and then direct him, if necessary, to the appropriate resource person.

INDIVIDUAL

This technique is equally effective with a student whom you suspect of having cheated on a test or an assignment. The teacher can ask her what he would see by doing an X-ray of her work: was more than one person involved in producing this work? It is always difficult for the teacher to address this subject: by means of this metaphor, it is easier to deal with the subject without assailing the student from the outset. She will probably be relieved by your approach and will confide in you much more easily when you have taken care to be tactful.

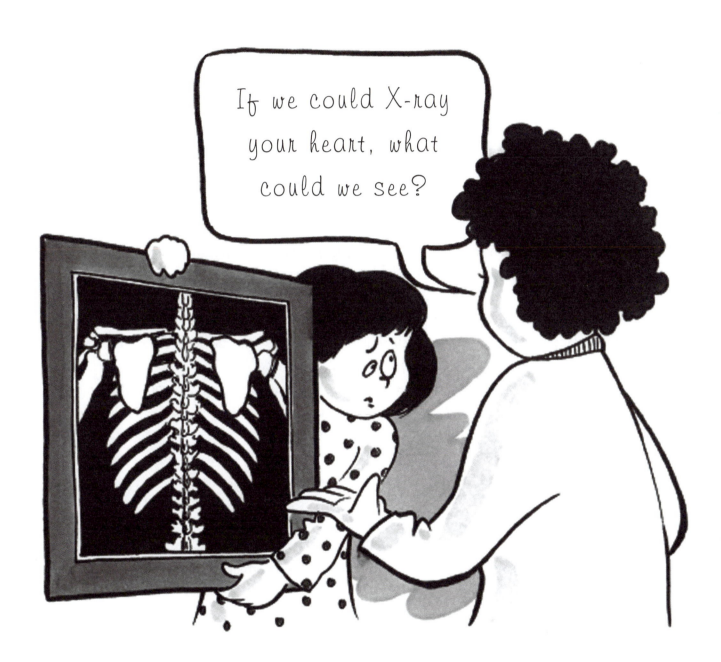

19

SPONGE

YOU WILL NEED

A scouring sponge.

INDIVIDUAL The teacher explains to the student that a sponge has the capacity to absorb a substantial quantity of liquid, but that when its full capacity is reached, no more can be added. At that point you need to wring out the sponge to empty it completely, so that it can once again soak up other liquids. In the same way, in class, when he lets himself be overcome by too many things that preoccupy him, he quickly reaches his full attention capacity and his ability to absorb information is full to the brim—his brain is already too full. How can he wring out his mental sponge, so that it is available to receive new information? What worries does he need to free himself of, at least temporarily, in order to be attentive? From a problem at home? From an argument with a friend?

INDIVIDUAL With a student who has failed a test, the teacher may ask, for example, if the sponge had absorbed the information, or if, when the information was given, a worry or distraction was taking up all the room.

INDIVIDUAL If you suspect that a student might be being treated badly by one or several classmates, talk to the victim, asking: if I were to wring out the sponge that contains what you hear from your friends and classmates, what would come out? A clear liquid made up of encouragement and kind words, or a filthy, black liquid containing insults? The younger the child, the more you need to offer a choice of responses to allow him to be specific about his thoughts.

INDIVIDUAL   The student can also use this metaphor to evaluate her choice of friends and their influences. Have her ask herself about what she would like to absorb in her life in the long term. For example, if she hangs out with young people who are drug users, her sponge will also end up absorbing alcohol and drugs: is this really what she wants to soak up now? And in two years? And in ten years?

20

FREEWAY

This technique will help the teenager to draw up a balance sheet of his current behaviors so as to become aware of their consequences.

YOU WILL NEED

A sign bearing the number of a freeway in your area that is familiar to the student and that you can make or reproduce from a photograph.

INDIVIDUAL Ask the student if he knows which direction, for example, highway 20 West heads. In your discussion, underline that by taking a highway and following it without deviation, you arrive at a precise destination. In the same way, the road that he is following currently will lead him inevitably somewhere: can he identify the direction and say where it will lead him? For example, if he doesn't do his school work and falls behind, can this road lead him anywhere else than to failure or, at least, to extreme stress during the end of year exams? If he is a drug user, where can this type of behavior take him? To a chronic addiction? A criminal record? If he uses disrespectful language toward his teacher, his family, and adults in general, how will he manage to develop trusting relationships that would make him feel an equal with them? In this way, examine with the teenager the roads that he frequents and if he plans to follow these paths all the way to the end.

21

Master key

PURPOSE This technique is intended to reinforce the student's self-discipline and his aptitudes for success.

YOU WILL NEED

A key that you can say is a master key.

 **CLASS** You will immediately obtain the attention of the group if you claim that this key allows you to go anywhere in the school buildings: a master key gives access to all the rooms of a building and accords complete freedom to the holder. In the same way, everyone can develop master keys that will open a multitude of doors right now and in the future, including, for example, discipline, perseverance, concentration, and the ability to adapt—in particular, to adapt to different people in the class. Emphasize that these keys cannot be bought and each person must forge their master keys for themselves. Ask the students if they devote time and attention to this blacksmith's work. Do they already possess the elements needed for making these keys? Have they already produced some good results? What else do they need to do in order to have fully finished master keys?

TIP

The heart box

This technique is intended to reinforce the cohesion within the group by improving the empathy and attention to others of each student.

This box will be exclusively reserved for positive comments addressed by name to the students in the class. They can include such things as congratulations for the student who controlled himself better and disturbed the others less, encouragement for the particularly shy student who is preparing for an oral presentation, and other similar remarks. The authors of the comments do not need to identify themselves. You can also participate and ensure that there are little heartening notes for those who really need them.

22
BIG STONES

PURPOSE This technique allows the student to draw up an inventory of his priorities and to identify the disruptive factors that prevent him from putting his priorities first in his daily life.

YOU WILL NEED

A clear glass jar, several big stones, as well as small pebbles, sand, and water.

■ INDIVIDUAL ●●● CLASS

It is recommended that you perform this technique in front of the students—rather than just telling them about it. Talking about it will certainly bring results, but children's brains (like adults, in general) are better able to retain information that recruits several neuronal zones. When sounds and images are joined with words in a single experience, several sensory centers are activated and process the information. It is easier to remember the essence of material that is recorded in several channels and is available in several regions of the brain

■ INDIVIDUAL ●●● CLASS

The teacher presents a clear four-liter jar with a large opening at the top. Delicately, he places large stones one after another in the jar and fills it up to the top edge. He then asks his students if the jar is full, to which they will obviously reply, "Yes." But the teacher then takes another container, previously hidden behind his desk, full of small pebbles, and pours this into the jar with the large stones. Again, the teacher asks his audience, "Do you think that it's full this time?" The students will obviously say, "No"—they won't let themselves be tricked two times in a row! The teacher then adds another, a large container of sand, and another, of water, so as to completely fill the jar, before revealing the moral of this experiment. If you don't put in the big stones first, there's no room for them later. Consequently, we need to identify the priorities in our lives before adding activities that may delay or prevent their realization. The biggest stones, naturally, represent work or schoolwork, while the smaller ones symbolize games and distractions—that is, activities that can compromise the attainment of academic objectives if they take up all the available space.

The discussion that follows should lead the student (or the class) to reflect on what disrupts the pursuit of her goals and about what she puts in her "life jar" first. Her friends? Her love life? Does she leave herself open to family worries? Does she blame her teacher for all sorts of things? School? Does she devote more time to having fun, playing on the computer, and going out than to her studies?

Getting the shy ones involved

This technique is intended to establish a foundation of positive experiences for shy students, to enable them to gain a minimal degree of confidence in themselves.

Shy people are excessively uncomfortable when you ask them to explain their point of view point-blank. Without time to prepare, the inadequacy of their thoughts further increases their fear of speaking and often causes stammering and jumbling of words. To enable them to train themselves to overcome this fear and get involved in discussions with more confidence, first, ask the question of the whole group, waiting for each student to think about and write down their response. Then ask the shyest members of the group to read what they have written on their paper. By doing so, you let them succeed in clearly expressing an articulated opinion in front of the group, thus creating the opportunity for a first confidence-building experience of public speaking. Evidently, by repeating this exercise, progressively reducing the preparation time—and then cutting it completely—you reinforce this new skill in your shyest students.

23

FILTER

PURPOSE This technique is suitable for discussing a problem of rejection or denigration with a young person overwhelmed by negative comments from his family or peers.

YOU WILL NEED

A coffee filter, two glasses, water, various bits of trash (cigarette butts, dead insects, and other small, unpleasant things).

● INDIVIDUAL ●●● CLASS

While pouring the water into a glass, the teacher explains that a healthy and kind person brings healthy elements to others—compliments and constructive remarks that are comparable to pure water. The teacher then adds to this water the bits of trash, explaining that there are other people (even family members) who, for reasons of jealousy, anger, or because they are aggressive, stressed, tired, or simply clumsy, say damaging things that do not necessarily correspond to their true thoughts. The more repugnant the potion becomes, the stronger each student will react to the question, "Who would like to drink this water now?" and the more effective the results of this technique will be. The teacher will then go on to say that, in life, it sometimes happens that we agree to drink this type of toxic and disgusting potion, by accepting and swallowing negative comments that come from brothers, sisters, parents, and friends who say unpleasant things in the heat of the moment. It's impossible to feel good after having drunk such a revolting cocktail. It's absolutely necessary to filter the words of other people to distinguish their real thoughts from those remarks provoked by emotion or fatigue. The teacher then passes the mixture through a coffee filter and purifies it, letting only the water pass through to the second glass, as a mental filter would let through only constructive comments. She then hands out an unused filter to each student who needs one (meeting them individually) or leaves them visible in a corner of the classroom as a reminder of the lesson to those living with this type of difficult situation.

24

Magazine

PURPOSE **This technique is intended to help "distracted dreamer"-type students develop their ability to concentrate.**

YOU WILL NEED

A magazine, the main subject of which is of particular interest for the student you are working with.

 **INDIVIDUAL** Showing the student the magazine, ask him if he is more likely to linger over the advertisements or the articles. Clearly, when we pay too much attention to the ads, we miss the essence (the information contained in the articles). Then compare his behavior at school with reading the magazine, by drawing a parallel between the ads and his distractions in class, then between his studious attention and the in-depth articles. It will then be possible, when you are moving through the rows during an exercise, to ask him discretely if he is flicking through advertisements or if he is reading an article. By taking his memory back to the subject of your conversation, you enable him to quickly re-center himself and help focus his concentration on the work at hand.

TIP

Video

To diversify your teaching methods while increasing their effectiveness through a multisensory approach.

After showing a video, present the students with a series of questions that will allow them to discuss what they have learned and understood. This will ensure that the new knowledge is more firmly anchored in their minds. The visual approach, richer in meaning than words alone, will prove far more effective if you have introduced the students to the contents of the video beforehand, and if you follow up by frequently mentioning the images seen together.

25

CD-ROM or DVD

Using these symbols, which represent readily available sources of information, this technique allows the student to define models of ideal behavior.

YOU WILL NEED

CD-ROMs or DVDs.

●●● CLASS By announcing that a CD-ROM or DVD entitled *The Best Student* has been recently launched on to the market, the teacher then asks the group what sort of information would be featured on the cover and what would be the headings in the table of contents. To help the students consider the ways of improving their performance, specify some of the main headings: attitude toward the teacher; schoolwork; involvement and participation in class; relationships with other students; clothes and physical appearance; and so on. Then take the time to ask the group if the CD-ROM or DVD would mention that you should always be perfect at everything? Discuss with them the need to set realistic goals that take into account the variations in performance. You should also emphasize that it is sometimes failure or less satisfying results that maintain and stimulate our motivation to work harder and give the best of ourselves.

26

Tokens

PURPOSE **This technique enables effective intervention with the boisterous students in the class.**

YOU WILL NEED

Different color tokens; each token constitutes a "right to an error", the significance of which varies depending on the color (trivial, medium, serious).

INDIVIDUAL

Boisterous children are often very marginalized by the class as a whole and receive disparaging comments and criticism more frequently—this exacerbates their excitability, fear of the teacher, and their boisterousness. From the other side of the classroom, the teacher who is constantly interrupted during lessons by this student often develops an irritability toward him that is likely to explode at any time. Offer this student a realistic number of tokens, according to your knowledge of his present level of agitation. If, for example, you have to speak to him an average of five times a day, don't give him just one token, give him six, in such a way that from the beginning, he can have the opportunity not to use them all, which enables him to begin counting on a positive feeling (likewise for the teacher!). Rather than being scolded in front of everyone with progressively more scathing remarks—particularly toward the end of the day when fatigue starts to make tension build up—you simply take a token, without saying anything: the gesture alone sends all the necessary messages ("You are bothering me and disturbing the concentration of the other students. Pay attention, you only have four tokens left!"). Moreover, you allow the student who finishes the day with two unused tokens to feel pride in having been able to control himself more than usual, which gives him the necessary motivation to improve further and the desire to experience that confidence-building feeling more often (a new feeling for him).

CLASS

This technique can also be applied to assignments to be carried out at home. In elementary school, the younger children fear being heavily punished when unforeseen circumstances prevent them from doing their homework as they should. Explain to the group that, first, you require that each student completes his homework and studies as best he can. Then, specify that you understand, however, that at certain times there may be some unexpected obstacles that interfere with getting their assignments done. As a result, everyone

will receive a token for each session—or month, or week (the younger the child, the shorter the interval should be). When a student arrives in class without having done his homework, you take his token, without punishing him. The child knows that the next time, there will be consequences for this breach. Generally, the group as a whole will pay attention to not losing its stock of tokens and you will receive better collaboration from each of them.

SUGGESTION

In your evaluation of the number of tokens to give your students, follow the 2 for 1 rule: first, estimate how many tokens you would need yourself (consider your own small lapses due to tiredness, distraction, and such) and multiply this by two—your students have less experience and discipline than you, don't forget!

27

CURTAINS, BLINDS, OR DRAPES

PURPOSE **This technique can reactivate the attention of students and actively encourage their participation, particularly at the end of the day, when tiredness or low interest levels prompt them to remain withdrawn.**

YOU WILL NEED

Use what you have in your classroom, depending on whether the windows are dressed with curtains, blinds, or drapes.

● INDIVIDUAL ●●● CLASS

Completely close all the curtains, emphasizing to your students that it is now completely impossible to see outside; when you open them, they will again have access to the view of the schoolyard or on to the road. Then explain to the students that, in the same way, some of them attend class with the blinds shut. In that state, they don't understand anything the others say, much less the teacher, because their vision of the world outside themselves is obstructed. How can they open their internal curtains to see once again what is around them, to better perceive the actions and reactions of others, to be ready to receive and integrate new knowledge? Also point out that when the curtains of the classroom are drawn, those who are on the outside cannot see in. In the same way, when a student keeps his internal blinds lowered, no communication or exchange with others is possible.

28

A GLASS OF WATER

This technique aims to encourage and reinforce the thirst for knowledge among those who show little interest in a given subject or for school in general.

YOU WILL NEED

A glass of water.

● INDIVIDUAL ●●● CLASS

Show a student a glass of water, asking him how thirsty he is (a little, a lot, or not at all) and stress the proportional relationship between this level of thirst and how much he will drink. The thirstier he is, the more he will want to drink; the less thirsty he is, the less he will feel the need to drink. The exact same thing applies to school, between his interest in lessons and the quality of his learning. The less thirst for learning that he has, the less he will take in the information and the less efficiently he will integrate it. On the other hand, the thirstier he is to learn, the greater his desire to access new knowledge and deepen the knowledge he receives. You can support him in his search for ways to increase his level of interest. Besides the reasons connected to the particular subject you teach, you can point out that success is socially well accepted and recognized, that often it initiates positive and constructive—even laudatory—remarks from parents, and that it usually gives you greater self-confidence. In itself, this intervention—reinforced by occasional reminders of your discussion (like placing a glass of water on the desk of the student, for example, and saying, "I think you may be thirsty today.")—is enough to awaken better attention from the student. If needed, keep a pitcher of cold water on your desk, either for filling the glass that you give to one or several of the students, or to signify to the class that you will have a lot of new knowledge to offer them today.

29

PLANT

PURPOSE
This technique is intended to reinforce the cohesion of the group and encourage its growth.

YOU WILL NEED

A plant, preferably a seedling.

●●● CLASS

Compare the plant to the whole group, explaining to the students that they too will be growing during the course of the next year. Just like the seedling—which will grow well, develop strength and vigor, and produce beautiful flowers if it receives enough water, sunlight, and care—the growth of the class can also be supported and looked after. This care translates into attention that everyone gives to one another, through prompt, relevant interventions; enthusiastic participation in group activities; and so on. If all the students decide to act as healthy contributions toward the growth of the class, it will grow in strength and harmony. Clearly, at the beginning of the year it's difficult to tell the good shoots from the weeds. A new group has just sprouted, but you all still need to get to know and discover this new group, to get past the distractions of the early period when everything is new and good work habits aren't yet established. When the seedling is well rooted, this means that each is capable of controlling themselves better, so as to concentrate better without disturbing the others, bringing them collaboration and support instead.

30
PHOTO ALBUM

PURPOSE   **This technique activates the synergy of the group and reinforces empathetic aptitudes.**

YOU WILL NEED

A photo album.

●●● CLASS   Show the class the album, explaining that we usually choose to put in an album the best photographs of our most precious memories of events, trips, or visits. In the same way, you will ask them to describe what they would decide to keep in their class album, at the end of the week, the month, the semester, or the school year. The brain is a machine that constantly produces images of what it experiences. Each student, therefore, holds diverse images of what he has experienced in class, but it is possible for you to have an influence on what he decides to retain. By asking him to sort through his recordings, you can rectify the memories that he chooses to keep. If, for example, he only retains information that is negative or destructive for him, you can help give him access to a reserve of positive images of the class. Share with the group the best moments recalled by their classmates of all of the happy, pleasant, and constructive events that might have been forgotten without this group recollection. This exercise will also promote social maturity in the students, who will learn to discern what is important and what is not for each of their classmates, thus developing a greater empathy as well as their ability to understand and accept differences.

Impact Techniques using OBJECTS that require the student's ACTIVE participation

Here are some additional suggestions using objects, but this time they require more participation on the part of the student ... as well as on yours! In general, due to the fact that these techniques are recorded experientially, they yield greater benefits than a simple demonstration.

Impact Techniques using **OBJECTS** that require the student's **ACTiVE** participation

WHITE BOX AND BLACK BOX

The white box represents a time when the student feels good, in full control of his potential, his aptitudes, and his abilities. The black box represents, on the other hand, states of tiredness, depression, anger, that is, the times when he doesn't feel good at all.

YOU WILL NEED

A white box and a black box, of the same style and size, which can vary according to your needs (from the size of a passport photo to that of standard paper).

This technique enables a precise understanding of the student's state of mind to be obtained while actively involving him. Children as well as teenagers often experience difficulty in translating their feelings, but through the mediation of objects like these, they can show concrete representations of the well-being or disquiet that they are experiencing—without having to use language. Likewise, they can quickly identify a relationship between their state of mind and their productivity, as well as between their appreciation of the teacher and the amount they learn from their classes. The exercise therefore leads to a greater sense of responsibility in the student.

INDIVIDUAL The student will be invited to stack the boxes so as to translate as closely as possible how he is feeling now. If, for example, the black box almost entirely covers the white box, the teacher will easily understand that the student is not feeling good at all. It is then possible to explain to him that this box represents what he feels and not what he is. It is part of him that is not really or completely him as a person; a negative part that deforms and distorts his reading of reality. Therefore, it's important that, when he realizes that he is going through a negative period, he not make weighty decisions, because the black box is always a bad advisor and the decisions that he might make under its influence would often be regrettable. When the white box reappears, this signifies that there is no longer a bad influence interfering: at that time the decisions that he makes and the actions that he takes really correspond to what he would like to do.

●●● CLASS This technique will help the teacher to maintain a better class dynamic. The teacher distributes on each desk a black box and a white box. When the students come into the classroom, they arrange their boxes according to their mood. The teacher who notes that a student has placed the black box on top will be able to interpret the student's nonchalance, inattention, or apathy as something other than a mark of aggression or disrespect. Knowing that the student is having a bad day, the teacher will have less of a tendency to question him or scold him, and, by so doing, to inflame the situation and increase the tension. Moreover, when the white box is on top, the teacher can give the student the chance to feel more valued within the group and can encourage his contribution more.

●●● CLASS The teacher who notices that a child almost always places the black box on top will recognize that she is probably struggling with a major problem that she needs help with. It is then easier to approach the subject with the student and to direct her to the services of a professional who will know how to give her appropriate support during this difficult period in her life.

●●● CLASS This technique proves to be even more effective when the teacher agrees to open up to the exercise honestly, by positioning her own boxes so that they can be seen by the whole class. Not only does this transparency and frankness from an adult present a healthy example to the students, but they will also be able to put their empathy to use. Acknowledging that their teacher is having a bad day, they will not judge her so harshly, understanding that adults also encounter difficulties—and they will doubtless also contribute more willingly to the activities in class.

32

STICKY TAPE

PURPOSE **This technique is intended essentially to favor "repairman" behavior among students, by making them aware of the negative consequences of some of their actions and by demonstrating to them that they have the ability to repair what they have broken.**

YOU WILL NEED

A roll of sticky tape.

● INDIVIDUAL ●●● CLASS

The teacher will ask the student to explain what sticky tape is used for (sticking two things together), and then ask her to actually stick together the pieces of a torn-up sheet of paper, using the tape she gives her. Clearly, if the teacher anticipates that the student will refuse to collaborate, it is useless to propose this part of the exercise, because the effect would be just to increase her resistance even more. As far as possible, however, try to have the student perform concrete actions, because learning through the actions of the body is extremely effective. In addition, the new knowledge will be anchored more deeply than if they were acquired through intellectual effort alone. When the child or teenager has stuck the pieces of paper together, underscore that she has just shown you that she knows how to use the right tool to repair a broken object. If, for example, she has insulted a classmate, you can then point out to her that the insult damaged something else and that she possesses what is needed to repair it. Stress the analogy, mentioning that you know that the friend was really hurt by the remark and that, in the same way as she has just repaired the torn paper, she is also able to stick the pieces back together with her friend—using the best tape for these circumstances: a sincere apology. Every damaging action can be repaired with the right type of tape—whether work to be done, apologies to give, a present or a kindness to offer—which the person we hurt or offended will understand to mean that we are sorry for what we did or said.

 **INDIVIDUAL**  **CLASS**

If you are talking to a teenager, it might seem that he takes this little lesson lightly. But make no mistake, because he has participated in this exercise, the image of the restorative act will stay in his head and gradually take hold—and will most probably strongly influence his reactions in the days following the intervention. Should the opposite be the case, if he does not display the desired behavior, you can always, from time to time, leave a roll of sticky tape on his desk or give it to him with a knowing smile (and not by putting pressure on him to act the way you think appropriate).

33

Post-it Notes

PURPOSE This technique allows you to help the student who finds it difficult to assert himself to gain greater confidence and better self-mastery.

YOU WILL NEED

A pad of self-adhesive notes, such as "Post-it" notes.

INDIVIDUAL During your discussion with the student, write down on a Post-it note the strengths and qualities that you identify (or want to reinforce) in him. Sign the list, drawing a heart, a star, or a hand at the bottom, and ask him to stick the note to his chest, his arm, or his foot. For the whole day, he will wear these qualities that you have recognized in him. This will help him to keep them present and demonstrate them in his behavior. The adhesive note constitutes a symbol of the teacher's constant presence, which will make him feel encouraged and supported.

You will be surprised to see how, for example, a note of this kind can comfort and reassure a student in the last year of high school who is nervous about delivering an oral presentation. Your support can also accompany the student outside the school setting, when you suspect that he is going through a difficult period at home and you show him your encouragement with a personalized note. This technique reinforces the quality of your relationship as well as his trust in you.

Forming teams

To establish better cohesion within the group.

The secret to reinforcing cohesion within the group is to increase the number of tasks to be done in small groups (teaching activities, participation in setting up the classroom etc.). After being paired with one or two other students for an activity, however brief, the student will have learned to know the other student(s) better, to become closer, and to respect them more—which clearly will contribute to strengthening the ties within the whole of the class.

To ensure the diversity of the composition of the groups and to favor the blossoming of understanding between students, you can give each one a number, making up two or three series. If, for example, you have 30 in the class and you want to create groups of three, divide the class in three series of ten students, with each student given a number from 1 through 10. Ask the three number "1's" to sit together, the three number "2's", and so on. If you are teaching history, give each student a letter to spell out the subject. The "H's" will then form one group, the "I's" another, and so on. At the beginning of the year, when the students do not know each other very well, this exercise immediately creates a comfortable and respectful group dynamic.

34

Playing dice

PURPOSE This technique lets you sensitize the students to the differences that make each member of the group unique. It can also be used to help students who indulge in too much wishful thinking to realize that reality is quite different from what he imagines. Additional applications include making the student responsible for his choice of attitude when he faces different challenges, and also to make the shy child aware of the necessity of making choices and acting on them.

YOU WILL NEED

Playing dice.

CLASS Distribute one dice to each of the students, asking them to roll the dice and tell you the result (How many of you got a 1? a 2? and so on). By comparing the numbers obtained, you will demonstrate that in one class it's impossible for everyone to get the same results. In the same way, each of them obtains different academic results and formulates his or her own opinions and ideas. To ensure that the class dynamic is healthy and harmonious, everyone needs to know how to respect the differences of the other and to try to see how these dissimilarities can enrich our perspective and our comprehension—rather than judging others because they rolled a different number.

INDIVIDUAL When working with a student who thinks he knows and understands everything, and, as a result, thinks he does not have to make any effort at all in lessons and studies, the teacher can ask him to throw six dice and get 6's on all of them. This result is obviously impossible to achieve on the first attempt. Encourage him to start over, again and again. Finally, underline that just like he needed to roll the dice many times and persist and continue doing so, he needs to have the same behavior in class. If he wants to master and absorb a piece of information as perfectly as possible and to improve himself in a field worthy of his potential, there is no other way than to continue his efforts in a constant and sustained manner.

INDIVIDUAL The dice can also represent different facets of a person. Ask the student to roll the dice and comment on her result, saying, "Do you think that because you threw a 3, it means that the 6 or the 1 don't exist?" Then explain to her that she also shows, depending on the circumstances, a more positive or negative attitude toward the lessons in class or to a particular situation. Point out that it is always possible for her to react differently and show another facet of her personality. Ask her if she puts her best side forward or if she lets things "fall as they may" when in a group discussion, or when she fails a test or an exercise, or when she needs to prepare for an exam.

INDIVIDUAL To help the shy and reserved child take his place in the group, the teacher will ask him to shake the dice, but without ever letting it drop. While the student is doing this, the teacher will begin to draw a parallel between this perpetually irresolute action and the fact the he also often delays in making decisions. When he thinks too much about the consequences of his participation in class, about the best way to express himself, and other such worries, he never gets around to taking the first step, to taking action … or to taking his place in the group. Help him realize that, if the dice isn't tossed, he gets no (0) results. Yet as soon as the dice hits the table, he has the chance of getting at least a 1 and maybe a 6! In the same way, by taking the risk and moving forward, he has a good chance of having a more worthwhile experience than he'll have by remaining immobile and uncertain, cultivating his fear of the judgment of others.

35

POLYSTYRENE CUPS

This technique will eloquently demonstrate to the student who is having problems with schoolwork, or is not very interested in school, that his enjoyment of learning, and his success, are directly proportional to the energy and effort that he puts into them.

YOU WILL NEED

Several standard-size polystyrene cups and a larger cup filled with water.

■ INDIVIDUAL

Set out as many polystyrene cups as there are "departments" in the young student's life and clearly label them so as to optimize the visual impact of his perceptions: recreation (one cup for these activities as a whole or, if necessary, one cup for each type of activity: soccer, skiing, skating, video games), family life, his relationship with his pet, school, friends, television, and perhaps another cup for his very closest friend. Next, give the student a cup filled with water, which represents his energy reserve. Ask him to pour a quantity of liquid into each cup equal to the amount of energy that he devotes to that activity. The result of this distribution will probably show that most of his time and attention is devoted to leisure activities and friends, while the "school" cup got only the last trickle of water. From this, the two of you may now understand why he is having problems with schoolwork and perhaps even has a chronic lack of interest in it. The less we invest of ourselves in any given sector of our lives, the less pleasure we derive from doing the activities associated with it, and the less we want to get involved in them. Depending on the student, it might be useful to perform this exercise replacing the various life "departments" by the various classes, to help the student understand that those subjects in which he invests nothing of himself are also those that cause him the most problems. End the exercise by asking the student to redistribute the water in the different cups in a way that better meets the requirements of his schoolwork for the following week, while still allowing him to devote time to his favorite leisure activities or to the classes that he is more comfortable with. By adopting this more forward-looking approach, you'll lead him to anchor his resolutions by preparing himself more effectively to carry them out.

SUGGESTION

You could replace the poly-styrene cups with wooden blocks labeled as the "depart-ments" of the student's life, and ask the student to sort them in priority order accord-ing to the importance that he assigns to each of them in his life.

Computer   Friends   Skate   Math   English   Family

36

PLAYING CARDS

PURPOSE The purpose of this technique is to make the student aware of the effort he is actually making, or which he should be making, within the context of his school life.

YOU WILL NEED

Several decks of playing cards.

●●● CLASS   Place several decks of cards on a table, face up. Ask the students to gather around the table and explain to them that success in school requires the collaboration of various cards; one of these "cards" is the respect for common rules. Explain to the students what some of those common rules are, and then ask them to select the card that represents the degree of importance that they assign to such rules. Clearly, an "ace" or a "king" indicates a high degree of attention, whereas an "8" signifies a somewhat variable and haphazard respect for the rules, and a "2" represents a total indifference to this aspect of school life. Each student should select the card that represents his attitude. They needn't show their cards to the other students, as this is a self-assessment exercise concerning certain aspects of conduct. According to the criteria for success that you identify, you can then make use of the symbolism in the cards by associating them with various attitudes, such as, self-discipline, the ability to seek help or to offer help to others, the ease with which a student asks questions whenever any information seems unclear, how willing a student is to do the schoolwork and to make the necessary efforts to reach his goals etc. At the end of the card-selection period, each student will review his or her own set of cards to assess the likelihood of their having a successful school year, and to identify those cards/attitudes that should be improved in order to further increase their chance of success.

● INDIVIDUAL   When working with an individual, proceed in a somewhat similar manner, first by identifying the subject matter that you feel is causing the student difficulty, and asking him to select his cards. What card does he hold that represents his relationship with others, or a particular school subject? You may then develop a more subtle approach by

designating certain cards yourself to emphasize the student's strengths. For example, he may have selected a "4" for mathematics, but you may show him that he has an "ace" that he is not using. Therefore, it is less a matter of exerting all of his efforts to improve, than it is to assert his strengths more openly by playing the right card every time that he makes a contribution in class or does his schoolwork.

● **INDIVIDUAL**

An alternative technique consists of placing the playing cards face down on the table and asking the student to turn up a "3". It would be amazing if she were to find it on the first try; she should therefore continue, proceeding by trial and error, until she finds this card. You can then use this exercise to accentuate the following lesson: what occurred in this game also occurs in her learning process in school. She may occasionally get the right answer, but to be sure of achieving that each and every time, she should review, repeat, and assimilate the subject matter that she has just learned in order to know exactly where to extract the new information from among all of the facts that she knows. Of course, the technique will work more effectively if, during the practical exercise, you allow the student enough time to get to know where certain cards are found in the deck (an "ace", a "king", a "queen", and a "jack", for example). It will then be easier for her to conclude that by familiarizing herself with a subject, she will manage to find the right answers more easily during the next evaluations or exams.

What is your classroom rules respect card?

37

Qualities List

PURPOSE This technique, which is suitable for any age group, is a very powerful reinforcement exercise designed to intensify group cohesion. It should be offered to the class once or twice a year.

YOU WILL NEED

One sheet of blank or lined paper per student.

●●● CLASS Ask each of the students to print his last and first names at the top of a white page and then, slightly below that, one of his positive traits. Collect the sheets and redistribute them at random. Each student should then write down one quality on his classmate's sheet before passing it on to his neighbor, so that by the end of the exercise, everyone shall have printed a positive comment about each of his classmates. After the redistribution of the "Qualities list", you can ask the students to silently read their personal list of qualities, or to stand up and read it out loud in order to fully appropriate the positive traits that the others have recognized in him (during which time the others should listen, after having turned their own sheets upside down on their desks). In either case, this exercise profoundly affects each student, who realizes that the others think well of him and specifically associate certain qualities with him. You will notice afterward a new attitude in your group's dynamics, which will translate into spontaneous outbursts of friendliness, helpfulness, and cooperation, fostering a better teaching environment.

38

SCREWDRIVER

PURPOSE **This technique allows the students to examine how they behave in their interpersonal relationships (whether on their own or in terms of the group dynamics), by making them aware of the need for them to adapt their approach to the different personalities of their classmates and teachers.**

YOU WILL NEED

A full set of screwdrivers (Phillips, square drive, flat-bladed etc.) of various sizes, screws matching these different types of screwdriver, and some pieces of wood for class experimentation.

●●● CLASS Ask the students if a square-head screw can be used with a Phillips screwdriver. By having them actually conduct the experiment, you ensure that their entire beings—mind and body—participate and record the message that you want to convey to them. That message is, evidently, that, unless we select the right screwdriver for each type of screw, our efforts will fail. Then draw the parallel between this requirement to match the right screw with the right screwdriver and the students' way of communicating with others. Using impolite and aggressive language is like using a flat-bladed screwdriver with a Phillips-head screw. Clearly underscore that every individual may be compared to a different type of screw. Consequently, we need to develop our "screwdriver" potential as fully as possible if we want to form connections and relationships with other people in ways that suit their diverse personalities.

Generally speaking, respect for others, the ability to listen to them, and the capacity to acknowledge their feelings before talking about ourselves—these abilities together represent a type of screwdriver that allows us to effectively convey our thoughts and to address the other's heart with great versatility. Indeed, all types of screws are responsive to this way of communicating. In your demonstration, you may illustrate the traits of the "all-purpose relational screwdriver" by referring to events that occurred in the classroom and past experiences, in order to help the students identify what screwdrivers they are already using. You can also present specific examples that indicate what you will be expecting from them in the future (words, sentences, and attitudes indicating respectful interrelationships).

39

A SHEET OF PAPER

This technique is used to draw up a balance sheet of the quality of the student's attention toward his various concerns in order to adjust, if necessary, the amount of energy and time that he devotes to each one. Unlike technique no. 35 ("Polystyrene cups"), which relates to the student's behavior, this technique allows him to work on the content of his thoughts or the way in which his mind functions. Choose the technique that is best suited for the student with whom you are working, as well as the nature of his problem.

YOU WILL NEED

A sheet of paper.

INDIVIDUAL

The sheet of paper should be used to represent all of the student's thoughts. Cut up or tear the paper into sections so that the size of each piece represents the persistence or the frequency of the thoughts that the student entertains. For example, you can ask a teenager who is preoccupied by a secret confided to him by a friend (an unwanted pregnancy, a sexually transmitted disease, a bad drug experience etc.), and unable to free himself of his obsessive thoughts, to write down on each piece of paper the name of each thing he is worried about, obviously noting the biggest concerns on the largest pieces of paper. It will then be easier for him to grasp that his mediocre school results cannot improve because they have been relegated to the smallest piece of paper—demonstrating concretely he is devoting only a very small part of his powers of concentration to school work. Thus, he will realize the importance of "re-deciding" for himself those sectors to which he truly wants to devote his energy and his thoughts—that is, in those activities that are constructive now and for the future, rather than squandering them on questions that cannot be answered or in problems that he cannot resolve. Although offering comfort and support to his friend is important and beneficial, exclusively devoting the best part of himself to this would be nothing but

a waste of his potential. The exercise will be effective even if you are not very precise in the identification of what each piece of paper represents. What matters is that the student himself can get a realistic idea of the way his mind is functioning, and also that he knows that you will remain available to help him and, if need be, advise him.

Mediators

This technique permits improvement of class management in the short term and, over the somewhat longer term, the development of the "social responsibility" dimension of the emotional intelligence of your students.

Select a student, or form a committee composed of 3 or 4 students, who will act as class mediators and will be responsible for management of classroom discipline. The fact that you are entrusting this task to the students naturally makes those selected feel more accountable. It not only reinforces their self-confidence and prepares them to perform an active and voluntary role in their adult lives, but also ensures that instructions will be followed more closely, since a peer is for-

mulating them. It is important to select new mediators frequently during the course of the school year, so that everyone in class has an opportunity to experience this supervisory role. Since every student will have the responsibility of overseeing the proper functioning of the classroom, they will be more inclined to follow the rules that one of their classmates now has the task of enforcing. To ensure optimal cooperation, conduct a collective exercise to establish the rules at the beginning of the school year. If the entire class has agreed that a particular instruction helps to promote a favorable environment for learning and concentration, it will be easier for them to mutually keep themselves under control.

40
PENCIL

This technique allows you to make the student aware of the required sequential order of the preparatory steps that he needs to take in order to successfully perform certain activities.

YOU WILL NEED

A lead pencil that has never been sharpened.

INDIVIDUAL Ask the student to write his name using this pencil, even if it has not been sharpened. The young person will likely reply that there is no point in trying, because the pencil must first be sharpened before its lead tip can be used. This statement then provides you with an opportunity to point out that, in the same way, some things in life must be done consecutively and in the right order: work before leisure, concentration before an exam, apologizing for and correcting our mistakes before restoring trust in a relationship and continuing to interact with another person, and so on. You can reactivate this metaphor when, confronted with a recurring behavior that needs to be improved, you ask the student if he has properly sharpened his pencil. This is a more understanding way of asking him whether he has done his work properly before allowing himself some relaxation, which will avoid him being on the defensive and you becoming angry. Elementary-school teachers may use this technique to induce their students to organize their desks, take with them what they will need to do their homework, and collect their clothes before leaving the classroom.

41
Radio

To show how ambient noise or inattention adversely affects the learning process.

YOU WILL NEED

A radio.

●●● CLASS

The radio volume should be fairly loud (but warn your colleagues in other classes ahead of time!) to cover the sound of your voice. Ask the students to repeat what you told them while the radio was blasting: naturally, it will be hard for them to do so. You can either let them guess the lesson to be learned from this exercise or clearly tell them the message to remember: when there is too much noise in the classroom, the essential information is not understood, since it cannot be heard. It's therefore important to keep noise levels down so that each student can distinctly hear what you are saying.

●●● CLASS

Leaving the audio volume at its normal level, constantly change the radio stations for a few minutes. Then ask the students whether they understood anything that was broadcast over the radio. Draw a parallel between this and distracted attention. Alternating a few seconds of listening to what the teacher is saying with a few seconds of looking at the classmate next to her, followed by a few seconds of thinking about the next recess, is like switching radio stations. No message can be retained and no learning can occur. In contrast, remaining mentally focused is like tuning a radio to only one station, which makes it possible to understand the information that the radio broadcasts, while at the same time saving energy. You should also explain to the students that quickly switching back and forth exhausts the mind because it has to jump from one subject to the next without being allowed to focus.

42

CHALK, LEAD PENCIL, FELT MARKERS, AND BALLPOINT PENS

PURPOSE This technique is designed to improve the student's attention by making him aware of the fact that his learning performance depends upon how well he listens.

YOU WILL NEED

Chalk, lead pencils, felt markers, and ballpoint pens.

● INDIVIDUAL ●●● CLASS

Supervise the group as they participate in the following experiment by asking the students to successively write on a sheet of paper using a chalk, a pencil, a ballpoint pen, and a felt marker. Next, ask them to try to erase the various things that they have written. In the case of the chalk, whether used on a blackboard or on paper, the marks they made are easy to wipe off with a chalk eraser, or even with their hands. For the pencil marks, they have to use a rubber eraser to get the same results. The ink from the ballpoint pen is hard to erase, but they can still cover the letters with some white correction fluid. Finally, the felt-marker ink is usually indelible and marks so deeply—especially if the line is wide—that it even leaves an impression on the back of the sheet of paper.

Next, compare these different types of markings with the "mental marking" through which the concepts that you teach in class are imprinted—or not!—in the students' minds. Using the "distraction chalk", whatever is written—however clearly and legibly—is instantly erased. With the attention level of the pencil, the information is retained for a while, but any new activity quickly rubs out the memory of what had been recorded. The ballpoint pen, which corresponds to more sustained attention, allows a new concept to be registered on a deeper level, but the best marking is still left by the felt marker, which allows the students to really improve their grades and permanently imprints what they have learned in their memories.

Finally, ask the students to think about what means they might use to achieve this type of marking in their memory. The mere fact of having undergone this experiment, even if no particular method is found, will have the effect of activating each student's mental processes to

significantly increase his or her attention span—provided that they have the ability to adequately record and process the information received. To reinforce the impact of this exercise, give the student who may need it a short message made with a felt marker consisting of the words "Good Morning" drawn in bold letters. From this allusion to the shared experiment, he'll understand that he'll have to try harder to remember the lessons that you will be teaching that day. To pass on the same message to the group, suggest that the students "grab their memory marker", because you are going to tackle a very important subject and they should pay close attention.

Class to the rescue

This technique encourages each student to be more involved in the group and orients each student toward playing an active role in school life. At the same time, this approach allows the student to set his own goals—which he shall reach more enthusiastically than if you had imposed them.

Three or four times during the school year, set aside fifteen to twenty minutes during which the students—whom you have asked to form subgroups—will be responsible for preparing class activities. For example, they could come up with ways to help those classmates who are having difficulties in preparation for the next exam, in order to promote the success of the class as a whole. Or they could plan an enjoyable activity to celebrate the end of the school year, or any other special activity. By allowing them to be actively involved and to engage their sense of initiative and their creativity, you will observe that they will tend to draw closer to you and to dream up projects with the goal (in part) of surprising you. It goes without saying that these activities will require all of the students' support and participation—even more so than when planning field trips or group projects suggested by the teacher—however imaginative they may be!

43

PUZZLE

PURPOSE

To encourage each student to have a better attitude regarding group behavior during the entire year. In addition, this technique can be used to increase the students' awareness of how important each student's contribution is to a group project.

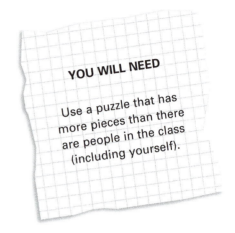

YOU WILL NEED

Use a puzzle that has more pieces than there are people in the class (including yourself).

●●● CLASS

First, distribute a piece of the puzzle to each of the students, putting aside the extra pieces. Then describe the activity to be performed by setting the common goal: to create a picture together in which each student will play a role and contribute whatever he can. Those who manage to place their piece in the proper position may then pick up another piece—but only one—in order to complete the puzzle. Make sure that you directly participate in this exercise, since you, like the students, are a part of the group's school life. To conclude, point out to the students that, just as they worked together to assemble this puzzle, they all help to ensure the group's harmony and success. You can make them aware of how important their individual contribution is by removing a few pieces of the puzzle and pointing out that a picture can only be enjoyed when it has all of its parts. Without each student's attention, interest, cooperation, and participation, the "class picture" would also be incomplete. But when each person tries to get along with others and is responsive to his classmates, the classroom can become an environment that ensures the best possible learning conditions. You may also reassure them by underscoring the fact that, just as each piece has its proper place in the puzzle, each student contributes his own special gifts to the group.

ELASTIC BAND

This technique makes it possible to tackle a problem of stress that the young person puts on himself, either through negative obsessive thoughts, an unhealthy perfectionism, or through the fear of judgment of others. It can also be used to deal with tension caused by a student's stress-inducing behaviors that provoke aggressive reactions from other students or wear out his body (excessive alcohol or drug use, insufficient sleep, hyperactivity etc.).

YOU WILL NEED

An elastic band made of fabric or rubber.

INDIVIDUAL Ask the student to hold the elastic band so that there is no tension on it and then to show you, by stretching the elastic band, the level of internal tension he feels when he engages in certain behaviors. For each item that you mention, or that you ask him to state, the student should apply and maintain a certain level of tension on the elastic band until he physically feels the effect—in his arm muscles—of the continuous stress to which he is subjecting himself. You can begin the exercise with, for example, the tension level that results from using disrespectful language with the teacher or with school administrators. Increase this initial tension level by making it understood that such attitudes automatically have consequences (withdrawal of privileges, the end of a collaboration, the loss of trust, threats of punishment etc.), all of which increase his stress level even more whether or not he is conscious of it. Next, boost the degree of internal tension even higher by pointing out his indifferent and careless attitude toward his schoolwork or his exams: what effect does the possibility of a test or a presentation have on the elastic band?

The first part of this experiment ends when the elastic band is stretched to its maximum degree, the second part then reverses the process, as you ask the student to relax the tension in proportion to the constructive attitudes that lessen his inner tension. For example, if he hands in his work on time and is proud of the result, or if he spontaneously and willingly

contributes to a group activity, how will these attitudes affect the tension of the elastic band and, by analogy, his internal stress? It is particularly important that the student experiences the benefits of relaxing the tension in his body and that he is able to physically contrast the slackening with the tensing. Don't forget to leave the elastic band with him, so it will act as a reminder and enable him to continue to think about this issue.

Scale of 0 to 10

The purpose of this technique is to help the students realize what their frame of mind is in class, and to help them develop an improved self-awareness.

Ask the students questions, such as: "On a scale of 0 to 10, tell me how comfortable you are with yourself? ... with your classmates? ... with your teacher?" "How much did you like this class?" "What number would you give for your pride in your work?" "What rating would you assign to your day's work?" The latter questions will allow you to show the students that their degree of interest is directly proportional to the extent of their involvement in learning activities—which will inspire them to become more deeply involved during the next class.

Still using a scale of 0 to 10, regularly ask your students to tell you up to what point each is willing to assist the class today. This very simple question will help them to become more conscious of the fact that their attitude can influence others and to exhibit behaviors that will let some of their classmates—those feeling less motivated or more tired than they are—to feel more at ease in the group.

OFFICE SUPPLIES

PURPOSE The purpose of this technique is to encourage better planning of school activities and more effective concentration.

YOU WILL NEED

Paper clips, chalk, erasers, pencils, rulers etc.

● INDIVIDUAL ●●● CLASS Gather all of these objects, then ask the student to sort them and arrange them by category. When he is done, emphasize how much easier it is to find what we are looking for when objects are maintained in their most logical order and grouped according to their purpose. Make certain that the student also makes some positive comments about the benefits of keeping things in proper order, then draw a parallel between this process and preparing his school assignments. In the same way that he arranged the objects on the desk, he should now organize and classify his schoolwork according to a schedule or calendar, by planning a succession of various steps, not by considering everything that he must accomplish as a single block. Not only does this way of looking at things generate a lot of anxiety, but it eventually proves to be unproductive, since it interferes with his concentration.

For example, it is hard to solve math problems if our mind is preoccupied with personal problems. Stress the fact that no one is a prisoner of his thoughts: he can control his by forcing himself to stay focused on a given subject, and by conscientiously applying himself to complete one task before doing something else.

The same technique can be used as needed to provide guidance to a student who was teased during recess, and is upset over it, by giving him a short mental classification exercise. What occurs on the school playground stays on the school playground; when he enters the classroom, nothing that has occurred outside of the classroom can keep him from concentrating.

46

School Desk

This technique illustrates the need for students to look for information or assistance in the place where they are available.

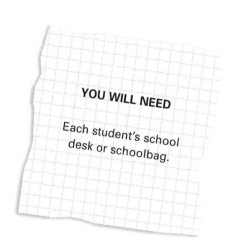

YOU WILL NEED

Each student's school desk or schoolbag.

■● INDIVIDUAL ●●● CLASS Ask the students to take out of their school desk or their schoolbag various notebooks and books, or even several sections of the same document. Markedly exaggerate the number of items that you ask for until their work surfaces are totally overloaded. Next, comment upon the activity by emphasizing that they knew where to find each type of document because they had put them in their desk or bag themselves. On the other hand, it would have been a waste of time to look for a one-hundred-dollar bill there. Similarly, certain things and certain information should be looked for in the places where they are available. For example, it would be pointless for one student who is having an argument with a friend to seek comfort from someone who would only take his part. That would not help the situation—to the contrary, it would only make it worse. Likewise, if a student needs the services of a specialist (special-education teacher, speech therapist, educational therapist, psychologist etc.), neither the student's parents, nor the teacher, nor a friend can really provide him with adequate help—the only one who can do that is the person who has been professionally trained to help him overcome his problem.

BALL

This technique may be used to illustrate the concept of reciprocity in interpersonal, as well as group, relationships, or to explain conflict dynamics.

YOU WILL NEED

A ball.

INDIVIDUAL **CLASS** Select a student in the class with whom you will toss a ball back and forth, then ask him to stop throwing it back to you whenever he chooses (you can also ask two students to perform this exercise). Tell the entire class that as soon as the student stops throwing the ball, the game is over. Clearly, both partners must participate in order for the game to continue. Similarly, when conflicts or differences of opinion arise between two people, at least one of them must stop "throwing back" criticisms and disparaging remarks at the other person; generally, the second player will end the dispute a few moments later, as he gains nothing by continuing to squabble on his own.

INDIVIDUAL **CLASS** Students can also learn another lesson from this exercise: in order for a relationship to last and to thrive, there must be an exchange between the two people involved, which means that they must collaborate in some way. When one of them extends an invitation, the other should usually respond to it. If only one of the players habitually throws the ball, but the other doesn't know how to throw it back, or doesn't want to, the first person is very likely to soon grow tired of it and stop wanting to play.

On the educational level, you can also use this technique to explain to the students that you are throwing the class many balls every day by communicating large quantities of information to them as you teach. They, too, can enhance the group's performance by throwing the balls back to you in turn, by ensuring that their assignments are neatly presented, by actively participating in class, making appropriate comments and raising pertinent questions, or by coming to you after class to offer their suggestions and constructive remarks.

Cut Flower

PURPOSE This technique will serve as a point of departure to incite the student to reflect upon his attitudes toward school or his interpersonal relationships.

YOU WILL NEED

A beautiful cut flower.

INDIVIDUAL ● CLASS Point out to the students that as soon as the flower's stem is cut—even if the flower is perfectly lovely now, and despite any care we may provide (regularly giving it fresh water, sprinkling nutrients into the vase etc.) it is bound to wither and die. Similarly, when students "cut themselves off" from school by being absent—occasionally at first, and then more and more frequently until they drop out of school completely—their interest is bound to decline, or even to disappear. By maintaining contact with the school environment and staying connected to that reality, they preserve part of their interest in school.

INDIVIDUAL ● CLASS The effect of radically cutting off interpersonal relationships—which frequently occurs among youngsters who suddenly decide to stop having any contact with one another—is that it leaves a problem unresolved. In so doing, each of them misses an opportunity to learn and to grow, just like a living flower on its stem, which can weather storms—and sometimes even deepens its colors under adverse conditions.

BASKETBALL

PURPOSE This technique makes it possible for the student to view dropping out of school from a new angle.

YOU WILL NEED

A basketball and a hoop.

● INDIVIDUAL ●●● CLASS Invite the students to play a basketball game and to score points by making baskets. After a while, take the ball away, but ask them to keep on playing. They will immediately react by saying that this is impossible. Allow them to express their opinions on the subject: they will probably say that the game is boring and a waste of time, and that they cannot focus on the same goal like they could if they had a real ball. Next, draw a parallel between this game and cutting classes. School is like a ball in the game of life: when the ball is taken out, the game is no longer as interesting. The ball can also be compared to their graduation diploma: without it, there are many games we cannot play and doors that will remain closed to us. Therefore, to keep on playing the game, we must hold on to the ball, just as we must stay in school to preserve our potential for success and to gain access to a variety of work and social environments.

THE "SNAKES AND LADDERS" GAME

PURPOSE This technique can be used to explain to the students that life has its ups and downs. It certainly has its pitfalls, but it also offers some wonderful opportunities.

YOU WILL NEED

The "Snakes and Ladders" game.

INDIVIDUAL Start the discussion by mentioning that—in life as in this game—everyone encounters ladders that he can use to work his way up and advance more quickly, but there are also snakes that make him tumble, and give him the impression that he is regressing. Encourage the student to describe the ladders that he has already encountered in his life, and then tell you about the snakes that have made him suffer. For example, a student who has a great deal of potential, but who felt sick during an exam, couldn't perform as well as he expected. To help him keep his situation in perspective and regain confidence, show him that this is a snake in his path, but that—just as inevitably—a ladder will soon appear that will help him to advance even further.

Some major trials, such as parents divorcing, the death of a friend, a handicap, or an accident, often represent long "snakes" that cause the student to lose a lot of ground. You can revive his hope by assuring him that this problem has already made him stronger, and that he will come across "ladders" that will allow him to make up for lost ground and to make great strides in the future.

51

Explosive mix

PURPOSE   This technique will help the student recognize the danger inherent in the mixtures that he creates, or—to the contrary—make him realize that the effects produced by separate positive elements are increased tenfold when combined.

YOU WILL NEED

If you are unfamiliar with chemistry, ask one of your colleagues who specializes in this field to prepare for you a mixture that will produce small and harmless explosions.

● **INDIVIDUAL** ●●● **CLASS**   Conduct this experiment in front of the class while explaining to the students that by mixing two substances that are not dangerous in themselves, we can nonetheless cause an explosion. Likewise, some combinations of attitude can also produce explosive mixtures. For example, although class absenteeism, taking drugs, or hanging out with the wrong kind of friends can, in and of themselves, constitute fairly minor problems, combining them seriously worsens their harmful aspects, sometimes to the extent of blowing a young person's life to pieces.

● **INDIVIDUAL** ●●● **CLASS**   To use this technique in a positive way, combine, for example, a conflict situation with a sincere desire to communicate. This mixture will produce an explosion of understanding that may even lead to a reconciliation. Better yet, combining two positive factors will produce a spectacular explosion: focused attention coupled with hard work is certain to radically improve a student's grades.

Teacher's Desk

This technique is specifically intended to be used with students who—consciously or unconsciously—are experiencing academic or personal problems and need help.

YOU WILL NEED

Use your own desk—provided that it is very heavy. If it is not, select another object in the classroom that is hard to lift.

● INDIVIDUAL ●●● CLASS

Ask the student to lift your desk (provided that it is very hard to do so). Encourage his efforts for a while, until he gives up and clearly tells you that he is not strong enough to do it or that the desk is too heavy for him. You may then compare this experience with the difficulties that he is now experiencing. On his own, he cannot lift them or get rid of them; however, if he seeks help (and at this point you can indicate to him the person best qualified to help him), he will manage to solve his problems and to free himself of their weight.

53

DIMMER LIGHT SWITCH

This technique makes it possible to address the concept of individual or group discipline, as well as to gauge an activity's intensity (whether constructive or disruptive).

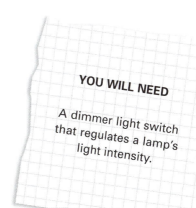

YOU WILL NEED

A dimmer light switch that regulates a lamp's light intensity.

 INDIVIDUAL CLASS

Begin by having the students experience concretely the variation in light intensity. Then discuss with the class the usefulness of such a device and the moments when it would be appropriate to use more subtle or brighter illumination. Among this technique's various applications, you can mention the noise level in the classroom, each student's concentration and attention level, and the speed at which a work assignment or task is completed. Whatever subject you may choose to highlight by comparing it to the dimmer switch, it is vital to make the students think about the concrete details that would characterize the reduced or increased intensity of the activity concerned.

TIP

Teacher's pencil

To help forgetful students remember instructions more effectively.

Regardless of the instructions that you want your student to remember and follow (such as, asking him to bring a particular object from his home to class tomorrow, or completing an assignment by a given day etc.), lend him one of your pencils or pens, and tell him that—if he will use it to write down these instructions on a sheet of paper, or in his assignment book, he will surely not forget it. This little "hypnotic induction" usually proves very effective, because you have made him focus on remembering the instructions.

54

CLASS DECORATIONS

PURPOSE This technique may be used as a starting point for a process of self-reflection on the quality of the thoughts and behaviors of the group, or of an individual student.

YOU WILL NEED

The various objects now decorating your classroom—whether or not you consider them of interest.

●●●■ CLASS Observe, with your group of students, the various items decorating the classroom, pointing out the objects that, as orderly and harmonious components of the room, make it more attractive, pleasant, and welcoming. In the contrary situation, explain to the students that the overall impression of coldness produced by the room can be specifically attributed to its lack of decorations, which make it look ordinary and impersonal. Similarly, if we want to beautify our relations with others—with our teacher as well as with our peers—we should give them a few decorative touches, such as constructive comments, compliments, or thoughtful gestures. In contrast, a relationship that we fail to decorate (by not talking to the other person or trying to contact her etc.), or to which we add ugly objects (arguments, insults etc.), often makes us uncomfortable and makes it hard to enjoy being together. Prompt the students to think about what actions they are taking to improve their interpersonal relationships, as well as those they might develop.

●●●■ CLASS This metaphor can be extended even further by discussing with the students the behaviors that enhance or mar the classroom. Their attitudes, their smiles, their kindness and politeness, their participation in class activities, the respect they show others all help to make the classroom warm and pleasant, while violent and contemptuous conduct, among others, makes the classroom a distressing and disagreeable place.

 **INDIVIDUAL** This analogy can also be used as a basis to discuss the student's inner "decor". What does he have on his mind? Self-destructive thoughts or thoughts that cause him pain and humiliation? Or, to the contrary, is he thinking words of self-encouragement, congratulating himself on his hard work, complimenting himself on his successes? Emphasize the fact that it is essential for him to "decorate" his inner life with pleasant thoughts if he wants to improve and enhance the quality of his daily life.

TIP

Wish list

This technique reinforces the development of empathy in each student.

According to Daniel Goleman, empathy is one of the fundamental components of healthy emotional intelligence. It not only helps to foster good relations with others, but also to build higher self-esteem. On a Friday, just before leaving the classroom—and even though everyone is in a hurry to leave—ask each student to express out loud a wish concerning a classmate. If you suspect that one of them may be overlooked by the other students, begin by expressing a wish yourself about that student. The wishes may vary, but should be based upon what the well-wisher knows about the other's pastimes: "I hope you have a good time with your parents in the country!" or "I hope that you have fun at your violin lesson and that you enjoy playing," or "I wish that you and your mother would never argue", etc. You will probably be surprised to find out that, when each student reaches out in this way to a classmate by paying special attention to him, the bonds of the entire group are strengthened considerably. And the more often you do this exercise, the more benefits everyone will derive from it, and the more enthusiastic about the game the students will be.

PARTY BALLOON

This technique allows the teacher to show the student a direct example of his mental activity, whether it is learning-oriented or troubled by counterproductive thoughts.

YOU WILL NEED

A party balloon inflated with helium that you have filled with confetti and decorated by drawing a pair of eyes and a smile on it.

● INDIVIDUAL ●●● CLASS

The confetti may represent many different things that normally float about in the minds of children—or adults! If you are using this technique to exemplify knowledge, approach the subject by saying that you know that they, too, already have several kinds of confetti in their heads. Then ask them the best ways in which to take advantage of what they already know, or to prepare to inflate their balloon by adding some new pieces of knowledge into it.

● INDIVIDUAL ●●● CLASS

If you decide to use the confetti and balloon as an analogy for the counterproductive thoughts that invade the student's mind, emphasize the fact that these thoughts (or too much confetti) uselessly weigh down the balloon, which eventually ends up crashing because it can no longer keep floating in the air. Furthermore, such thoughts occupy the space that new knowledge needs in order to be stored inside the student's head. How could the student sort out his thoughts or rid himself of some of his excess distracting thoughts?

 The confetti can also represent secret thoughts, which should not necessarily be shared, but which sometimes interfere with other brain activities. For example, you can advise the students to simply leave such secret thoughts at rest by refraining from stirring them up. While you explain this, hold the balloon very still. Then, shake the balloon in such a way as to make the confetti move around inside, in order to show that these thoughts disturb the calm, the concentration, and the availability of the mind that are needed to take in the teacher's instructions and lessons.

 INDIVIDUAL ●●● CLASS   Another use of this technique may foster moments of intense imaginative or intellectual activity. The balloon's movement would then symbolize an individual or group brainstorming session when looking for ideas, solutions, or answers.

TIP

Silent attention-getting signal

This technique will enable you to economize your efforts to get the attention of your students and make them focus on you in an amusing context.

Together with the students, decide upon a gesture that will signal the end of discussions during work in teams. For example, you raise your hand, which means that the current exercise is now over. When the students realize that you have raised your hand, they must each hurry to do the same thing. Because of the snowball effect, each student will see the signal from someone. Even if a particular student is not looking at you, she will get the message as soon as she notices her neighbor's raised hand. And since the signal is already associated with silence, it becomes easier for the students to comply.

You can also use intermediate signals to manage the various stages of a workshop project. For example, if you raise only one finger, you are indicating that the first part of the exercise is over, or that the first scheduled activity has just ended. By raising two fingers, you are signaling that it is time for the second part to start and so on. In this way, you can complete ten steps without having to say a single word!

56

CARBON PAPER

This technique allows you to address the issue of how students influence each other.

YOU WILL NEED

A sheet of carbon paper and two blank sheets of paper.

● INDIVIDUAL ●●● CLASS

When we use carbon paper, what we write on one page is also imprinted on the second page. Similarly, a person's behavior can sometimes influence someone else. If, for example, you suspect that a student is spending time with friends who have a bad influence on him, you can ask him what the others are imprinting on his personality. Before starting to hang out with them, he seemed to be interested in class and got good grades, whereas now his grades are plummeting and he is less and less attentive in class.

● INDIVIDUAL ●●● CLASS

You can also use this technique to demonstrate how constructive attitudes nurture good relationships. The compliments that we give someone else leave an imprint on her, just like "plus" signs are copied on to the second page. Encourage the students to think about the impression they make on others by asking them: What are you writing on their carbon paper? What marks are being imprinted on their classmates' papers? What good marks have they themselves received from the members of this group? Are some of those marks not so good? To make this exercise more personal, continue the process by asking each of them what marks you—the teacher—have imprinted on the student's sheet. Are they pleasant or not so favorable? What kind of marks does each student think he has imprinted on your page?

Different roll-calls

This technique is intended to enhance self-awareness.

When you check to see who is present in class, use a different roll-call method by asking each student to express his general feelings in a single word, number, sound, or gesture. This exercise, which Daniel Goleman recommended in his book *Emotional Intelligence I*, compels the student to increase his self-awareness. Choosing a symbol for his current state may help him to realize that—when he is not in as good a mood as usual—he does not enjoy his day as much, he finds class less interesting, and he will be more critical of his teacher. However, when he is well rested and in a good mood, he is

more easily engrossed by the lesson and appreciates the type of teaching that he is being given.

This technique acts as a signal to his classmates as well as the teacher. Because they know the student's general frame of mind, his classmates and teachers can adjust to his mood, which sometimes may even inspire some compassion that otherwise could not have been expressed. Moreover, this practice allows the teacher to notice whether one of his students is constantly ill-at-ease and gives him a basis for discussing the subject with the student, or for guiding him to the resource person best qualified to assist him.

57

A NAIL AND A WOOD BLOCK

PURPOSE This technique enables the student to grasp that the only way for him to fully assimilate a lesson or a behavior is by making repeated efforts.

YOU WILL NEED

Some wood blocks thick enough for the nails used to be totally driven into the wood. Each student should receive his own block to nail.

● INDIVIDUAL ●●● CLASS The nail driven into the wood block represents the student's perfect assimilation of what has been taught. Just as the head of the nail must be hit several times to drive it all the way into the wood, it is also necessary to make several efforts in order to really assimilate a new skill or a new lesson. In order to emphasize the students' efforts on a daily basis, give them the opportunity to hammer on their personal wood blocks when they have just truly applied themselves to a given subject. This action will show others, as well as the student with the hammer, that what he has learned is starting to take root in his mind.

Thanks to this technique, expectations become more realistic, especially among those students who are experiencing some learning difficulties. The depth of the nail helps the student to assess the progress he has already made and to more accurately gauge how much work still needs to be done. The technique can be used in the child's home environment, where his parents can assign a small piece of wood to each school subject, thereby helping the child to keep track of what he is learning through homework and lessons.

● INDIVIDUAL ●●● CLASS The wood block can also represent the acquisition of a new behavior or success in reaching a personal goal. If the targeted goal is, for example, to be more attentive in class, the student who feels that he has reached his daily goal because he has made real efforts may drive in his nail at the end of the day. He will soon realize that it is becoming easier and easier for him to pay attention, since driving the nail into the block has become a habit—a behavior that he has now assimilated and which he finds easy to practice.

LOUIS
Stay calm.

ERIC
Give his opinion.

JULIA
Be tolerant.

MONICA
More hard work in math

JORDAN
Devote more energy to a task.

58

LIGHT BULB

YOU WILL NEED

A lamp and a light bulb.

● INDIVIDUAL **●●●** CLASS During this exercise, discuss with the students what happens if the bulb is not screwed into the lamp, if the lamp is not plugged into the electrical outlet, or if the electric switch is in the "off" position. Even if the bulb has all of the potential energy it needs to provide a source of light, it cannot do so if one of these conditions has not been met. Next, draw a parallel between the electric bulb and the student's mental "light bulb"— the one that lights up inside the student to help him understand what is being taught in class. Like the electric light bulb, the comprehension process is sometimes interrupted by small problems. For example, despite all its capacity, that internal light bulb can't light up if the student's mind is not plugged into what the teacher is saying, when the student's motivation is in the "off" position, or when the method for doing the assignment is not appropriate for what is requested (in other words, the internal light bulb is not screwed in properly). Encourage each student to ask himself if one or more of these problems is preventing him from "lighting up" on what is being taught. Then you need to guide the student in his search for solutions so that his intellectual light bulb may—from then on—provide optimal light.

Happy memories

To activate some beneficial memory circuits in your students' minds.

The purpose of this exercise is to activate the student's production of cerebral endorphins. Since the brain does not distinguish between what it experiences for the first time and what it relives in memory, recalling a past experience generates the same physiological response as it recorded when the experience first occurred. When we remember an event, it is not just images that resurface, but also emotions and sensations.

On a technical level, this is how you should orchestrate this exercise, which—from start to finish—lasts about three to four minutes. You should adjust the time for this drill according to the age of the students and the topic to be considered (although 60 seconds is a reasonable average time). Ask the students to team up in pairs, then designate the boy or girl who will begin the exercise by using such prompts as: the oldest starts first, or the one with the longest hair etc. Pose one of the questions (listed below) to the group and let each student silently think about it for a few seconds. Then the first student gives his response to the question for 60 seconds, making the best possible use of the time allotted to him and being careful to tell half of his story or half of his ideas by the time he reaches the 30-second point. During this time, his partner listens without interrupting him, using nonverbal signals to show that she is paying attention, without encroaching upon the first student's "air time". After one minute, the teacher indicates that it is time to reverse roles, and the second student answers the question by presenting her ideas or memories to the first student, who now listens to her as respectfully as he was listened to.

As for the content of this exercise, you can use some of the following questions as your starting point, while insisting that each student explain why he answers the way he does: Can you tell the story of one of your accomplishments? Can you identify someone who has had a positive impact on your life? Who do you admire the most and why? What kind of person do you consider a "special friend"? What animal would you like to be, if you had the choice? Under what circumstances did you feel the bravest that you have ever been? What was your proudest moment?

In selecting your questions, the important thing is to adapt them to the type of activity that you want to encourage. For example, to help the students stop feeling anxious over a major exam, you can ask them to do this exercise while urging them to tell the class about a moment when they felt totally in control of themselves and in full possession of all their faculties. You will notice a very evident improvement in their work, since you will have stimulated, in their minds and bodies, the circulation of the ideal biological factors to face this type of test.

59

A DRAWING

PURPOSE **This technique enables the student** to understand how he is perceived by the group or by the teacher, and to become aware of how he is fulfilling his role.

YOU WILL NEED
Make three versions of the same drawing. In the first version, the object is not clearly visible, because it is only partially or lightly drawn. The second version is still incomplete, and the third drawing will be clearly recognizable because the lines are complete and very distinct.

■ **INDIVIDUAL** ●●● **CLASS** Ask the group to identify the object based on the first drawing. The students will probably be unable to do so, because too much information is missing for them to get an exact idea of what the partial sketch represents. From the second drawing, it is possible to tell what the object is, but certain parts of it are still missing and are only visible in the final version. This technique can be used when working with teenagers who regularly skip class. In order to improve your relations with the student, and renew his motivation for attending class, you can tell him that, to you, he is like the first or second drawing. Because you do not see him very often, you cannot understand him well enough to discover who he really is and to make a connection with him. By seeing him more regularly in class, you would be able to get to know him, to offer him help better suited to his real needs, and to maintain a closer relationship with him.

■ **INDIVIDUAL** ●●● **CLASS** With very young children (as with teenagers), you can discuss each student's level of involvement. The very shy student corresponds to the first drawing; the second drawing represents the student who occasionally participates in class (though only intermittently and unpredictably), while the third version represents the student who is committed and responsive, and who is attentive to others as well as to what is being taught. In this context, too, you can inform Type 1 and Type 2 students that it is hard for you to really know them and to discover their talents. Moreover, you can even stress the fact that students who don't take their rightful place within the group often experience low self-esteem, which generally translates into relationships that are unrewarding and disappointing.

60

CARDBOARD-MAN CUTOUT

PURPOSE   This technique is designed to make the students more aware of what they give and receive in their relationships with others.

● INDIVIDUAL ●●● CLASS   Ask each student to write, on a Post-it note, an insult that someone has said to him or her (such as, "you're a stink", "you're stupid", "you're a jerk" etc.), and come forward to stick it on the cardboard-man cutout, until the latter is completely covered with gibes. Discuss with the students how the cutout man might feel after receiving these comments. To help them think it over, ask them how they felt when they were called those names. Did they keep the insulting Post-it notes to themselves, or did they immediately stick them back on the person making fun of them? Did they then stick even more derisive Post-it notes on others? These questions are intended to make them realize that hateful remarks lead nowhere and harm both the person who receives them and the one who makes them. This type of concrete, "hands-on" experience will remain engraved in the student's mind and help prevent him from harboring such harmful attitudes. Moreover, once the insult-posting session is over, you can stress that the good characteristics and positive qualities of the cardboard man can't be seen anymore. What is visible is not the real person at all, but just a one-dimensional image distorted by remarks that may be untrue, or exaggerated, and that only concern one isolated event and not the individual as a whole.

Sparklers

YOU WILL NEED

A pack of
sparkler sticks.

● INDIVIDUAL ●●● CLASS

First, ignite a sparkler, letting the student know that it will only last 3 minutes. Second, cut one-quarter off another stick, then light it, while pointing out that the latter will obviously burn one-quarter less time. Continue shortening the next two or three sticks in the same way, and finish your demonstration by comparing this with the effects of taking drugs. At first, a drug dose produces euphoria that lasts a relatively long time. However, drugs have the particularity of quickly becoming habit-forming, which means that the same quantity does not provide the same pleasure—neither as long, nor as intense—as it did at first, because the effects gradually diminish, until there is barely a flicker. To re-experience the brilliance of the first fireworks, the dose has to be increased, which accelerates the student's drug habit and addiction. Finally, hand the student the last sparkler stick—the one cut off at the base—and ask him to think over his decision to use drugs.

Several factors may be taken into consideration when assessing behavior involving the consumption of drugs. Even if some students are outside of your immediate sphere of activities, as a teacher you nonetheless occupy a privileged position for intervening in a youngster's life—particularly if you already have a good relationship with him. By using a medium such as the sparklers, you can induce him to think about his problem, and the images from the exercise will impress him—all the more so because he will be moved by the fact that you concocted this experiment just for him, so that you could communicate with him and help him to think about his present life, as well as his future. By showing him your disapproval of his drug use, you are also indirectly showing him that he matters to you.

62

PITCHER AND GLASSES

The purpose of this technique is to make each student conscious of the fact that he is responsible for the spirit of the class, as well as the general atmosphere in the classroom, just as much as the other students are.

YOU WILL NEED

A transparent pitcher and glasses.

●●● CLASS

Give a glass to each student and place at their disposal some fresh water, coffee, ashes, cigarette butts, modeling clay, tissues, grass cuttings, dust, fur, and other refuse. In his glass, each student should prepare a mixture that matches his attitude in class, or his feelings about the group. Pure water—with its nourishing and cleansing properties— can therefore represent a feeling of general well-being or of great satisfaction with school. Grass can signify distractions, and the ashes, like the dust, can represent disruptions or negative reactions. Once everyone has prepared a mixture that matches as closely as possible his feelings toward the school or the class, collect their personal contributions in your pitcher. You can show them that all it takes to make the whole pitcher look cloudy is a single portion of murky water—just as it takes only one troublemaker to disrupt the whole class. Moreover, several doses of dirty water in the group's pitcher create a general unpleasant feeling, and make the students uncomfortable. Each student is thus made aware of how important the quality of his contributions to group life actually is. In order for the pitcher to be full of fresh water, each student must examine the purity of his contribution. If every student tries to prepare his personal mixture with wholesome elements, the contents of the pitcher can only be refreshing and pleasant for all.

CARDBOARD

PURPOSE **This technique uses an experience** that, by transposing a tense mental attitude into an uncomfortable posture, allows the student to physically experience—on a physical level, which makes more of an impact—the actual cost of his obsession.

YOU WILL NEED

A piece of cardboard and a black felt marker.

INDIVIDUAL The problem of obsession can take several forms in a young person's environment. An obsession may be indirect, and stem, for example, from a parent who is convinced that you are asking far too much of his child, or who believes that the direction taken by the school is not in the students' best interests. The child himself may be obsessed by harsh comments made to him by a classmate or an acquaintance during recess, and therefore be haunted by the fear of having to stand up to the other child. The teenager may be obsessed by drugs, alcohol, sex, or other temptations of adolescence.

Whatever form the obsession may take, it always prevents the individual who is experiencing it from making his best efforts and from applying his skills—intellectually as well as socially. In order to help make the child (or his parent) aware of how much of an impact his obsession has on his life, write the object of the obsession on a piece of cardboard, using a black felt marker: failure, injustice, divorce, fear of ridicule, fear of not being able to do things, or another concise description. Ask the student to hold the cardboard right in front of his eyes, so close that this is the only thing he can see, even if he has to squint to see the problem written on it. You can help him to understand that by staring only at the cardboard, and focusing all of his energy on the problem, he cannot see anything else. He is thereby cutting himself off from many aspects of his life—the more constructive and positive ones—which he cannot be aware of as long as he pays no attention to them. To demonstrate this, show him certain tools (paper clip, pencil, pencil case) and place them at his eye level, but behind the cardboard. Point out to him that, since he is keeping his nose glued to his problem, it is

hard for him to see what you are offering him. Draw a parallel to the learning aids that you present to him in class, which he does not use because he is still focusing too much on his problem. Finally, ask him to move the cardboard a few inches away from his face, and then offer him the same objects that you did previously. This time they fall within his field of vision, because he has now distanced himself somewhat from his problem. Stress the fact that he can now see many more objects than he did before, and that his situation is less painful. In fact, holding a piece of cardboard with both hands in front of the eyes eventually gets tiring and uncomfortable—and may even induce anxiety. Finally, make him realize that such discomfort can be easily lessened, because he has the power to push away the cardboard or to let it fall. He is partially responsible for his obsession and can therefore choose to focus his attention on other aspects of life and invest his energy elsewhere.

64

Investment Ladder

The purpose of this technique is to develop the student's capacity for self-criticism and to improve the quality of his involvement in the group.

YOU WILL NEED

Make a weekly school calendar that will also include the name of each of the students.

● INDIVIDUAL ●●● CLASS

Every day, each student should note on the calendar his degree of involvement in class activities by assessing his levels of cooperation, attentiveness, kindness and politeness, perseverance and tenacity, and other behaviors or attitudes. Make sure that you specify very clearly which criteria they must meet to earn a perfect score of "10" out of 10, or a "7", a "5", and so on. This daily exercise will oblige the student to become more aware not only of his attitude in class, but also of its repercussions on his grades, as well as on his relations with the teacher and his peers.

In order for this technique to be truly effective and enable young students to develop their self-awareness, the teacher must also evaluate himself as sincerely as he can. What is more, it will be your honesty and transparency that will qualify you as a model for them to follow as they develop their self-assessment skills. High school teenagers usually appreciate being treated like adults, so if the teacher makes a contribution to the exercise, and identifies with them by placing himself at the same level, they will interpret that as a sign that the teacher is acknowledging their maturity and they will value him all the more for having confidence in them. You are bound to notice an improvement in the quality and frequency of their cooperation in class.

65

ROPE

PURPOSE This technique is intended to be used with a student who cannot let go of his problem, which is preventing him from investing himself in the other areas of his life.

YOU WILL NEED

A rope.

INDIVIDUAL Ask the student to hold on very tightly to the rope that you are offering him because you will be trying to take it away from him. After this little "tug-of-war" exercise, ask the student to imagine that the rope represents the problem he is currently experiencing (divorce, failure, handicap, broken heart, a hurtful incident etc.), and tell him that you will once again try to take it away from him. Typically, the student will react in exactly the same way as he does in real life: if he tends to give up easily, he will let go of the rope; if, to the contrary, he usually firmly latches on to things, you will find it hard to win this match. Compare his attitude toward his problem to his way of refusing to give up in the game. To reinforce the impact of this exercise, take full advantage of every aspect of the metaphor by describing some of its consequences. For example, when he clutches the rope so tightly, he cannot hold anything else in his hands; he is investing a substantial amount of energy that he cannot therefore devote to any other area—including aspects of his life where it may be really needed.

INDIVIDUAL The rope can also be assigned a positive value, such as, a project that he will be as committed to now as he was before his problem. This might include such goals as to do better in school, to participate in a sports event, and so on. While he is identifying and defining this project, test his determination physically by pulling on the rope. If necessary, encourage him to hold the rope even tighter, in part to show him that he will need to be more tenacious if he wants to reach his goal, and in part to replace his previous tense attitude with a deliberately more active and determined one.

BACKPACK

This technique allows the teacher to concretely demonstrate the weight that some students are carrying on their shoulders.

YOU WILL NEED

A backpack.

● INDIVIDUAL ●●● CLASS

Rather than simply talking about the expression "carrying a weight on their shoulders", make the student experience this literally by getting him to carry a fairly heavy backpack. Specifically, tell the student that this is how you perceive him: as someone who is constantly bearing a very heavy weight on his back. Can he confirm or refute your perception? You will probably need to reassure him by telling him that you don't want to know what is in the bag—that is his property and he can share it as he wishes. He will be relieved to know that you are aware of his situation, and his uncomfortable posture, and he will even feel supported by the concern you offer. By using the backpack, you can help him to concretely gauge the physical and psychological cost of his burden. How is it affecting his performance in schoolwork, or in sports? What impact does it have on the fulfillment of his interpersonal relationships, his love life, or on his self-esteem? You can also ascertain whether he has the resources that he needs to help him lighten his load. Even if he answers affirmatively, take the time to make him list these resources and to suggest the names of other people who can help. If you want him to understand that you are willing to be a resource person for him, clearly identify the periods during which you would be free to meet with him. He will thus know that he has someone he can go to who cares about him enough to have conducted this little experiment, someone who is already concerned about him and will welcome him warmly if he should ever need help.

 **INDIVIDUAL** **CLASS** Depending upon the openness of the student with whom you intervene, you can perhaps address the nature of the weight he is carrying on his shoulders, not by talking directly about the secret (or secrets) that he is bearing, but by describing the backpack's characteristics. Exactly how much does it weigh? How much does each of its separate parts weigh? What color is it and what is its shape? Is it possible to jettison part of the load? Without knowing precisely what problem the student has, you can thereby obtain a few hints that will give you an idea of the scope of the problem.

TIP

Group statement

To help the student sharpen his self-awareness, and to learn to summarize and communicate his point of view. To be used frequently with the group, in a two- to three-minute format, at the beginning or end of your classes.

If you are reserving the last few minutes that you usually spend with the students for this exercise, ask them to very briefly tell the group one thing that they liked, or did not like, that happened during the class or during the day. When starting a period or a new day, the topic should be what they liked best about your previous meeting, or what they would like to do again today, or possibly what they found most enjoyable or entertaining about their weekend. You will thus give them an opportunity to express their point of view, and to exercise their ability to express their feelings succinctly, thereby giving them the opportunity to cultivate a priceless ability.

67

Pairs of Sunglasses

This technique can be used to illustrate how subjective each individual's perception of a particular situation can be.

YOU WILL NEED

Several pairs of sunglasses, with lenses of different colors.

● INDIVIDUAL ●●● CLASS

Each student has his own way of perceiving a given situation: when several students are involved in the same event, there are just as many "versions" of the story as there are youngsters. To help each student develop a sense of responsibility for the way he perceives things, as well as to help him develop a different way of seeing, have him try on several pairs of sunglasses with differently tinted lenses. Ask him to look at various objects and describe the differences he perceives between each pair. With the first pair of sunglasses, the light is more orange-colored; with another pair, the light is bluer, or darker, and so on. After he has experienced a variety of different lenses, ask him how he perceives the class now, or how he perceives you. The student should acknowledge that he has his own vision of things and that his way of looking at things is necessarily his own. This gives him a totally unique vision of what is around him, which may sometimes also imply that this vision is distorted. If he feels that you are always on his case and never stop scolding and watching him, help him to realize that other students perceive you quite differently: are his "glasses" distorting his vision of things? Without necessarily having to admit that his glasses distort reality, the student may nonetheless clearly express his perception of your teaching, your person, or any other subject that induced your intervention with him. Your discussion will allow you to readjust some of his false perceptions and, for your part, change certain reactions with regard to him.

TIP

Teacher—student signals and

This technique helps develop a positive complicity between the teacher and a student who has been rejected by his classmates, or who is momentarily going through a difficult time with his family, or who has health problems.

Develop a nonverbal language system with the student to whom you want to offer support. For example, if the youngster is having trouble keeping up with the lesson, he can place his hand in front of his desk and raise two fingers. To thank you for any special attention, he would raise four fingers. For your part, when you want to make sure that he is understanding the lesson, and that the pace is not too fast for him, indicate the number "3" to signal your question. What matters is that you both use your signals in such a way that the other students do not realize that you are using signals to communicate with each other. The student concerned, on the other hand, knows full well that you have personally sent him a secret message and will thus be more motivated to look at you and to keep paying attention, since you have created this system just for him.

Teachers who have experimented with this technique have not only noticed marked improvement in the child, but also have felt truly gratified to have found a way to offer practical support to a student in difficulty. And to know that one is truly helping those who need it the most—Isn't this one of the greatest satisfactions that a teacher can ever experience?

68

A TISSUE, A SHEET OF PAPER, AND A GLASS

PURPOSE **This technique allows the teacher to assess what defenses a student is using to protect herself against criticism and negative comments made by one or more tormentors and thereby better arm her to cope with these unjustified remarks and to renounce the role of victim.**

YOU WILL NEED

A tissue, a sheet of paper, and a glass.

INDIVIDUAL Ask the student to hold up, one by one, the objects listed above under "YOU WILL NEED". For your part, use a pencil to pass through the shield that she puts up to defend herself. When your pencil pierces the tissue, show the youngster that this type of defense does not really shield her from disparaging comments, which can too easily pierce her, hurt her, or tear her apart. When she is holding a sheet of paper, use the pencil more aggressively, simulating the destructive comments or insults that she may receive. Emphasize the fact that criticisms can damage anyone who wraps herself in paper armor. However, a pencil will never be able to penetrate a piece of glass (or wood). The glass armor therefore represents an effective defense against people who want to hurt her or who say hateful things. Then you can question her about the kind of defenses that will keep her safe from the aggressiveness or spiteful actions of others. How might she develop an even more effective defense? The simple fact of experiencing concretely the vulnerability of her defenses will motivate the student to develop better ways to protect herself in her relations with others.

INDIVIDUAL The thickness of the various materials used can also be compared to the way in which the student interprets the comments that she receives: both the tissue and the sheet of paper receive and totally absorb the blows ("Yes, I *do* look like a nerd ... everyone hates me for that."), but the glass and the wood resist the blows ("He's really mean", or

"She's just putting me down so that she can feel better about herself"). You can let the student keep a small piece of glass to help her recall what the exercise taught her, or even ask her to think about your discussion whenever she holds the glass in her hand, which will continuously reinforce her defenses against others.

● INDIVIDUAL
It is important to note that the shield of glass or wood is not meant to exemplify closing off social relations or an aggressive retaliation (which would be better simulated by using a knife or a very prickly surface). You may need to show the student several examples of the type of empathy and restraint that she must use in dealing with others in order to protect herself in a healthy way.

69

VARIOUS OBJECTS

PURPOSE **This technique will help students who are experiencing increasing rivalry to become conscious that they are getting ensnared in escalating dynamics that not only are troubling for them individually, but which are also disrupting the entire class.**

YOU WILL NEED

Various objects, preferably small.

INDIVIDUAL Ask the two rival students, who have been accumulating many negative remarks and rude replies, to come forward and take turns placing the objects one on top of another, until they form a pyramid. Initially, avoid comparing this experience with their behavior, but point out that stacking small objects, which in themselves may not be very substantial, can eventually create a big pile. Next, guide them toward the lesson behind the exercise, letting the realizations come, as much as possible, from their own comments. You can round out the discussion by underscoring the fact that all it takes is for one of the two rivals to stop placing objects on the pyramid for the other to also grow weary of the game and to stop playing.

If necessary—depending upon what you know about the students, and whether or not you suspect that one of them is capable of pursuing his little war on his own—emphasize the fact that if one of them continues to accumulate negative words and gestures he will become the only one responsible for his "mountain", since the other would have rid himself of the problem. It might be a good idea to review the facts and actions that set off and sustained this animosity between them so that you can help them to examine how their dispute developed. Help them recognize that their disagreement is not unsolvable: it is just a matter of each one taking back the pieces that he put on the pile by apologizing for each time he used bad judgment.

CLASS   You can use this metaphor in a positive way, by drawing the following lesson from the group's collective experience. All it takes is for each student to make his own modest contribution—a few efforts to be on time, to pay attention, to be open to the comments of others, and to always be available to help those who need it—to obtain a truly significant result for the entire class: a pleasant group environment that every student can enjoy.

PARENTS   This technique will also help some parents to understand that they need to also provide a better-supervised home environment for their child, and offer him more support. Everyone makes a contribution to the student's progress, starting with the youngster himself, his teacher, and his school. When all of the partners involved in the educational process—including the parents—contribute their efforts, the student learns more and integrates that knowledge more thoroughly.

LACED SHOES

This technique is specifically intended to be used with overprotective parents who may be hindering their child's potential.

YOU WILL NEED

A pair of laced shoes.

PARENTS

Speaking to overprotective parents is extremely delicate, because they are likely to be easily hurt or offended by your intervention. You must therefore proceed with caution and use active listening and paraphrasing techniques to first establish a trusting relationship. Firmly assure the parents that you know how important the child is to them, that they are constantly looking for ways to support and guide him in his development, and how lucky he is to have a mother and father who invest so much time, energy, and attention in him. However, you have an experiment to suggest to them that can be used to determine if the child is really getting the amount of attention and support he needs. Note that it is much less offensive if you conduct the exercise yourself. If you were to ask one of the parents to tie his child's shoes, the demonstration's impact could be much stronger, but such a gesture might provoke more intense and emotional reactions. So use your own shoelaces, and tie your left foot to your right foot, then get up and walk to show them how difficult it is to move around under those circumstances. You have to make tiny steps and cannot advance very quickly, nor go very far. In the same way, a child's limited autonomy does not allow him to progress at the same pace as others do, which inevitably hurts him because he feels deprived and fearful, since—unlike his classmates—he doesn't have the chance to experience for himself what seems so easy for everyone else.

In order to raise the parents' awareness of the actual impact of their attitude, do not hesitate to point out some of their behaviors that limit the student's autonomy. For example, you noticed that they had strictly directed him to choose a specific subject for his next presentation, depriving him of the initiative of finding a topic on his own that he would like to explore. Or perhaps you know that the student will not be able to take part in the year-end cultural exchange event planned by the class, or in sports events, because the parents are afraid of letting him go far from home. Encourage them to untie the psychological shoelaces on their child, starting—if need be—by the activities that are limited in terms of time and location, so that each member of the family may gradually become accustomed to relaxing this control.

Impact Techniques
using CHAIRS

How could we possibly overlook the primary teaching tool that you have in the classroom: the chairs? You will be surprised by all the possibilities that they can offer you, aside from their conventional role.

Impact techniques using CHAIRS

EMPTY CHAIR IN THE FRONT OF THE CLASSROOM

PURPOSE
Neuro-Linguistic Programming (NLP) often uses positive anchoring to enable the individual to make optimal use of his strengths in meeting the challenges that he encounters. Such an approach can provide effective support to students throughout their academic career.

YOU WILL NEED

An empty chair is placed in the front of the classroom, near your desk.

● **INDIVIDUAL** ●●● **CLASS**

A chair placed in the front of the classroom can represent a particular moment in the life of each student when he felt that he was functioning at the maximum of his abilities and accomplished something of which he is proud. First, ask each student to identify a moment when he successfully met a challenge—whether academic, athletic, artistic, or in any other area. To improve their recollection of that event, ask them to elaborate upon it as much as they can by prompting them with a few questions that each student should answer based on his own experience. What internal strengths had he mobilized? What was his physical condition and psychological frame of mind? Did he feel that he could call upon his full potential? Next, invite the student to mentally picture the person that he was on that occasion sitting in the empty chair facing the class. In so doing, you will induce the establishment of an anchor with this moment when the student felt—and knew himself to be—strong, steady, capable of fulfilling his own expectations as well as those of others. He can thus draw on his vital energies and cultivate his feeling of self-worth.

You can considerably reinforce the quality of your relationship with each of your students, and encourage them to feel like winners, by frequently touching this chair when you are working at the blackboard or moving around in front of the class. All of them will undoubtedly notice this affectionate and confident gesture that you personally convey to each of them.

Useless chair

> **PURPOSE** This technique may help students cope with the stress produced by inner conflicts.

YOU WILL NEED

A chair.

● INDIVIDUAL ●●● CLASS Students are often in conflict with themselves: one part of them wants to do his work, the other prefers to play; one part enjoys being in class, the other does not like being there. According to the description that the student gives of himself, ask him to designate a chair for each of the parts he has identified and to explore the motives and arguments for each. Why does this part want to work and do the tasks that are expected of him? What thoughts are going through the mind of the other part, which is trying to slip away and does not want to get down to work? After describing in detail each of his inner personas, the student will be asked to remove from the room the chair occupied by the part of himself that he would like to be rid of for a while. If you conduct this exercise with the whole class, you should remove the unwanted part of each student yourself, by taking the chair into the corridor.

● INDIVIDUAL ●●● CLASS If you use this technique to soothe the feverish and excitable part of the student, the outcome will not be as impressive. If the student is not always calm and relaxed, the reasons for his agitation may have a physiological basis, in which case, he will not always be fully in control of his energy levels. It would then be more effective to induce the student to choose between *behaviors* or *strategies*, rather than to reject a part of himself. If you want to urge him to favor a more moderate attitude, make sure he is capable of voluntarily disassociating himself from certain aggressive conduct that he tends to repeat.

CHAIRS IN VARIOUS POSITIONS

PURPOSE   The purpose of this technique is to make the student more aware of the behaviors he exhibits in class.

YOU WILL NEED

A different chair should be used for each of the positions that you want to deal with.

● INDIVIDUAL ●●● CLASS   Begin by placing the chairs in various positions: upside down to represent introversion, laid on its side to indicate nonchalance and laziness, with its back turned to the teacher to signify unwillingness to learn or to follow directions, constantly in motion to represent a student who cannot sit still, or in its normal stable position, with its legs planted solidly on the floor, to personify an attentive and focused student.

Now point to each chair-model and ask the student to identify those moments or situations during the day when he exhibits this kind of behavior. Help him assess the benefits and the drawbacks of each position, in order to induce him to sit down on the last chair, which—being very straight and sturdy—will prove to be the most beneficial for him.

Excellent memory

To provide conditions that foster optimal student attention and concentration prior to a test or an important assignment.

Ask the students to identify, among their acquaintances, someone who would get a perfect score in this test or exam (or who would feel perfectly relaxed and in full possession of his faculties before and after the test etc.) Next, have them reflect on this person's special abilities—those that would ensure his success. Then ask each of them to imagine that he or she is this person, and has all of his abilities, before they go to work. Obviously, the results will not be perfect, but this technique will help them to perform better and distinctly improve their grades.

74

SUPPORTING CHAIR

PURPOSE This technique is designed to give the student a feeling of self-confidence.

YOU WILL NEED

A chair located in the front, at the side, or in the back of the classroom.

● **INDIVIDUAL** ●●● **CLASS** Ask the students to imagine that this chair is reserved for someone who likes them very much, believes in them, and accepts them unconditionally: this person may be a parent, a friend, or a teacher. Some of the students may identify the chair with a deceased person, but the important thing is that the person be someone who truly matters to them. In any case, it is unnecessary—and even inadvisable—to name the support figure: his or her identity should remain a secret. By permanently placing a "support chair" in your classroom, you are setting aside a real space for a presence that will reassure each of your students—a presence that will make even the most anxious students feel safe, instill confidence in those who feel less secure, and create a calm environment, especially during test periods.

75

NEUTRAL CHAIR

PURPOSE This technique will help the student to be less introspective and preoccupied with himself, and to develop a new perspective on his own attitude or an event.

YOU WILL NEED

A chair.

INDIVIDUAL If a disagreement arises between you and a student, or if two classmates are finding it hard to get along—whether because of a misunderstanding or an unfortunate event—first, help the student to realize that, from the vantage point of the chair that he occupies, he has a certain view of things. Invite him to move to another, more neutral, chair that is not the teacher's or another student's, but rather that of an objective person who is able to see the situation as a whole, and consider every point of view. Ask him to describe to you how he assesses the situation while seeing both chairs simultaneously, that is, both versions of the situation. How does that change his understanding of the problem?

INDIVIDUAL This technique can also be applied to schoolwork, class participation, or any school activity in which you would like to see the student develop a more lucid self-awareness, as well as a desire to improve.

Impact Techniques
using MOVEMENT

In general, teachers and therapists are less inclined to use movements than objects: these techniques may require a little more audacity. However, being the very first senses to develop in an individual, the kinesthetic (movement) and proprioceptive (bones, muscles, and ligaments) systems are the most powerful. The results of these exercises, despite the laughter and discomfort that some students may experience, will therefore be outstanding.

Confucius said: "What I hear, I forget. What I see, I remember. What I do, I understand." The outcomes of techniques that call for experience and movement brilliantly illustrate this principle.

Impact techniques using MOVEMENT

INTERDEPENDENCE

PURPOSE
The effect of this technique is to increase the bond between the members of the group and make them realize how much they influence their classmates.

YOU WILL NEED

No supplies are needed for this technique.

●●● CLASS

Ask the group to form as large a circle as they can, while keeping a certain distance between each student. Describe this stage by comparing it to the early stages of the collective life in a group: each student keeps his distance and stays in his own world because he does not yet know the others and is hesitant to break the ice. If we want to create a pleasant environment for the class, each student must offer his hand to his neighbor. If you want to stop uncontrollable laughter and awkward feelings—particularly if you are teaching a high school class—distribute pieces of rope to all the students and ask each of them to extend it to the person next to him, thus avoiding physical contact. Continue by describing this stage as being that of respect: extending our hand to someone, or making a friendly gesture means that we are accepting the other person, not making fun of him, and we are considering his point of view. Next, each student should take one small step forward, which represents being punctual in class and when handing in assignments. Have them take as many steps as necessary to symbolize the various ways in which they can actively participate in class that you consider important: asking relevant questions at the proper moment, cultivating mutual helpfulness, having an open and friendly attitude toward others (teachers and students), and so on. As each step brings them closer together, you can point out that when each of them makes a contribution and cooperates as best he can, the entire group benefits from it. With each step, the bonds between them strengthen, they know each other better, and they feel closer.

Finish the exercise by asking them to return to their initial position while still holding on to the other person's hand or to the end of the rope. Then ask certain students to take one or two steps forward: they will thus experience what happens in a group when only some individuals truly make an effort while others refuse to take their steps. Each student will sense the

tension that this inequity produces within the group, and will be more likely to participate and cooperate because he will have realized that his idleness affects all of his classmates individually. Then, take a few minutes to let the students express how they felt when they were standing behind, "torn" between those who were not moving and those who were stepping forward, or when they were trying to take a step but felt pressured to stay back. Do they have any suggestions for preventing such feelings of indecision in class? Are they more conscious now of the positive or negative impact that each individual inevitably has on the group?

Steps of Unruliness

This technique can be used with students who disrupt the class, but do not yet merit suspension, to make them aware of the immediate and long-term consequences of their attitude.

YOU WILL NEED

No supplies are needed for this technique.

INDIVIDUAL

Have the disruptive student stand in front of your desk, facing you, and ask him to take a step backward or sideways (depending upon where the classroom door is located) each time that you mention an action he has taken that disturbed the entire class. For example, "When I asked you to stop talking to your neighbor, you kept on doing it, so take a step back (toward the door)." He will implicitly feel that he is distancing himself from you while getting closer to the door, thereby realizing that his behavior cannot be tolerated indefinitely and that it has unquestionably caused him to distance himself from you, and brought him closer to getting a suspension. If necessary, lead him physically, step by step, out to the corridor, and leave him there a few seconds so that he can completely grasp what the ultimate outcome of his current attitude will be.

Next, you can do something that will be very beneficial to him in the future: make him take a few steps toward you as you mention what actions he can take to improve his behavior. After this experience, he will be all the more motivated to replace his former habits with a new kind of behavior. Since this exercise involves the student's implicit memory—to his body, as well as his mind—you will not need to dwell extensively on the negative or positive consequences of the attitude that he now intends to cultivate. However, you should be very attentive when the moment arrives to acknowledge his least effort, and be sure to congratulate him verbally, visually (with a wink), or physically (by a tap on the shoulder), thus making certain that you are reinforcing the desired behaviors.

Musical signals
for getting attention

You may use any sound-producing object: alarm clock, cuckoo clock, toy, trumpet, xylophone, or a theme song from a TV program that you have recorded and can play on a tape recorder. In short, anything of a musical nature that does not sound like a bell ringing (normally associated with the end of the class). This is a lighter way to indicate the end of an exercise or evaluation. This tip will help your students' move on to other activities more quickly, especially if the signal produces a strange sound, because it will have made them laugh and relax for a moment.

HEAD-TURNING

This technique is specifically intended for students who are under the impression that, regardless of how many times they try, they will be unable to improve their schoolwork or their situation. Its purpose is to prove that—to the contrary—it is by persevering that they will succeed.

YOU WILL NEED

No supplies are needed for this technique.

● INDIVIDUAL ●●● CLASS

Ask the student to stand up very straight and turn his head as far to the right as he can, taking note of how far he can see before turning his head back to its original position. Next, have him repeat this movement several times, noting exactly each time the furthest spot he can see. Then ask him to tell you the difference that he noticed between what he saw the first and last time that he turned his head. Since a muscular phenomenon is involved, he is bound to see a little bit further each time. Draw the obvious conclusion: in this exercise—as in his assignments and homework—by trying a second, third, and fourth time, he will little by little improve his performance, and what seemed more difficult to him the first time, will gradually become easier.

79

THE CHAIR GAME

PURPOSE This technique is especially designed to be used with disruptive, agitated, and hyperactive students. Its purpose is to make them aware of the dynamics of their own mental functioning in order to help them to free themselves of it.

YOU WILL NEED

A few school chairs, including the one occupied by the student with whom you are doing this exercise.

● INDIVIDUAL Place five or six chairs in a circle and write on each one, using a Post-it note, what the student's main sources of distraction are, such as: "Nintendo", "What my friends think of me", "What I will do during recess"—in short, anything that relates to the student's inner world. One of the chairs will represent the school—more precisely, your lessons. To make the student conscious of the mental agitation that is troubling him, ask him to sit down on the first chair, and tell him that he will stay there the same amount of time that he usually devotes to this subject; however, immediately direct him to another chair, then another, and then another (do this 10 to 15 times), until he is completely dizzy from it. Make him realize that his mind is working in the exact same way, and he will admit that he cannot pay attention to your lesson or concentrate on his schoolwork, since he is constantly allowing himself to be distracted by several other thoughts.

Next, ask him to describe how his friends must feel when they are with him. Since they cannot follow the course of his thoughts, they cannot understand why he jumps from one subject to another, or from one game to another. Eventually, it makes them dizzy—just as this exercise made his head spin—and they will decide to avoid him. To help him better manage his mental activity, end the exercise by physically removing the distracting chairs from the classroom. Above all, make sure that the chair representing the sustained and focused participation in class is actually his own chair—the one he sits in every day. Thanks to the physical dimension of this experience, you will enable the student to concretely measure the demanding expenditure of energy that is involved in his current mental behavior and give him a real object that he can latch on to whenever he feels himself losing his focus: his own chair.

Be careful, however, about the expectations that you set for him: like all hyperactive children, his thoughts will continue to stray (we all do it!), so be sure to acknowledge and congratulate him for the least effort he manages to make at first, to build up and reinforce his new confidence in his ability to control his thoughts.

THUMBS

The purpose of this very simple technique is to make the students understand that the difficulty and discomfort brought about by change and new experiences gradually disappear when we voluntarily train ourselves to adapt.

YOU WILL NEED

No supplies are needed for this technique.

●●● CLASS
Ask the students to fold their hands and notice which of their thumbs is on top; next have them unfold their hands and fold them again, so that the opposite thumb is now in the uppermost position. Everyone feels slightly clumsy doing the second part of this exercise. Likewise, we also feel a little uncomfortable whenever we do something for the first time, and it can sometimes pose a real problem. However, with training and practice, it is possible to develop our abilities, and what was once a new skill can even become automatic. Whether it's a question of overcoming a problem with a particular school subject, or of adopting and cultivating a social or psychosocial behavior, the student will immediately grasp the concept that only through daily practice will he eventually manage to feel comfortable dealing with anything that is new to him.

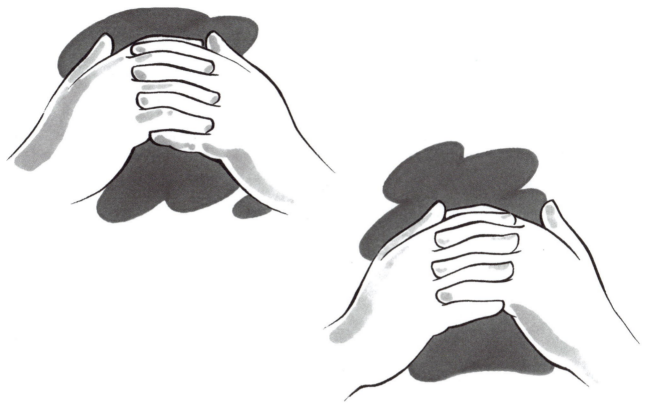

Positive group statement

To "come full circle" for a given period, induce the students to present constructive feedback about the events they have experienced.

Ask the students to identify the highlights of the last class, of the day, of the semester, or of the year. You can also assign a more relational topic by urging them to think about the most memorable moments that they shared with various people in the class, the teacher, or even other members of the school staff. By giving the students an opportunity to relive and name these positive moments, you are renewing the energy potential of those events and creating a climate of confidence and well-being in which each student feels comfortable and welcome to share with the group. In fact, all of these activities in which each student is called upon to speak and share his experiences in public imply and demand mutual respect, and foster attentive listening and empathy. These lessons on emotional and relational themes obviously exceed the limited scope of classroom discipline. However, by using such exercises, you will unquestionably achieve two goals, the most valuable of which for each of your students is to feel respected, listened to, understood and appreciated by his peers, as well as by you.

POSTURE

PURPOSE **This technique will help younger students realize that good posture enhances concentration, whereas the opposite—a poor body position—interferes with both the learning process and the completion of assignments.**

YOU WILL NEED

No supplies are needed for this technique.

●●● CLASS Ask the students to turn their chairs 180 degrees, stretch out one arm behind them on their desk, and write a few words. In order to manage this, they will be forced to assume an unstable and uncomfortable position. Tell them to hold that posture while you ask them: "Were you able to legibly write the words that I dictated to you?" "Do you feel comfortable in this position?" "Do you feel that your body is getting tired?" "Have you noticed that it's harder to perform well in this position?" By making them experience an exaggerated and inappropriate posture that prevents them from seeing what they are doing, you will help them realize that, to the contrary, by sitting up nice and straight, their body posture will make it easier for them to learn and work, rather than make them tired.

82
PUDDLE

PURPOSE This technique will help a student who is going through a tragic experience to understand that what is so painful to him now will gradually diminish.

YOU WILL NEED

No supplies are needed for this technique.

INDIVIDUAL Ask a student who, for example, has been humiliated by his peers, or has experienced a devastating academic disappointment, to watch for a puddle to form during the next rainy day, and to put only the sole of his shoe in the puddle (to avoid getting his entire shoe wet). He will notice, as he keeps walking, that the initially very distinct outline of his wet shoe sole gradually fades away to the point where it eventually totally disappears. Similarly, when a negative experience occurs in our life, it initially leaves visible marks, but as we go on with our lives they eventually disappear (at least the difficult part does).

TiP

A roast (without the banquet!)

To foster optimal group cohesiveness, and thereby minimize disputes and misunderstandings, while also helping each student to appreciate his classmates' best qualities.

You are no doubt familiar with this type of ceremonial tribute to someone that includes his friends and acquaintances drawing up a humorous list of all of his good qualities. Once every week, or month, plan a "roast" for one student in the group. It is not easy for students to perceive all of a classmate's qualities and express positive and warm comments without being embarrassed. Consequently, such an activity will not only prove invaluable to each of your students in the short term, but also in his personal and professional relationships throughout his life. In addition, while reinforcing the self-confidence of the student celebrated during the "roast", this exercise will teach him to appreciate and gracefully acknowledge favorable compliments or comments made about him, which very few adults are capable of doing without false humility!

CLOSED DOORS

This technique is specifically intended to be used with a self-deprecating student who is thereby inhibiting her own intellectual and social potential.

YOU WILL NEED

No supplies are needed for this technique.

INDIVIDUAL It is highly likely that the student's attitude is the result of a parent's demands and harsh discipline. You will thus not be able to totally eradicate this youngster's attitude, since she faces this critic on a daily basis. This experiment may be conducted with one of her parents present—but, as you may well imagine, there is no guarantee that he or she will cooperate with you. Tell the student that you have hidden a gift wrapped in blue paper somewhere in the classroom, in one of the cabinets or drawers, and that she may keep it if she finds it. As the student starts looking for it, follow her and prevent her from opening the cabinet doors or drawers, keeping them closed. She therefore cannot accomplish her goal, since you refuse to allow her access to those places that you had initially stated she could explore. Explain to her that by closing the cabinets and drawers, it is impossible to access the useful objects that they contain. Similarly, by keeping the drawers and doors of her mind closed, she is cutting herself off from realizing her own potential. She closes these doors whenever she accuses herself of being "stupid", tells herself that she is "good for nothing", or believes that she will never accomplish anything. By locking up the doors of her mind that way, she is bound to enjoy school less and less, and what was once possible for her will actually become impossible: when an ability is not applied or exercised, it eventually gets rusty and becomes unusable.

84

DIFFERENT PERSPECTIVES

PURPOSE
This technique specifically applies to parents who refuse to take the teacher's point of view into account, but persist in believing that their child behaves as angelically in school as he does at home, and refuse to accept any critical comments about their offspring.

YOU WILL NEED

No supplies are needed for this technique.

PARENTS

Hold any object in your hand and ask them what they see: your respective descriptions will differ, since you do not see the object from the same angle. Ideally, you should use a book with entirely different front and back covers. This experiment will help them realize that although your perspective differs from theirs, it is nonetheless totally valid. The truth about the child's character consists of a combination of your two views—and even that of others. You will find it easier to obtain their cooperation from this point on, since you have not repudiated their way of viewing their child, but instead have persuaded them to combine their perception with yours for the purpose of helping the child to improve.

TOY CARS

PURPOSE
This technique is intended for students who need support but refuse to accept any help.

YOU WILL NEED

A toy car.

INDIVIDUAL

Take a toy car from which you remove two wheels. As you push the car around on top of your desk, tell the student that you are perfectly aware of the fact that he is not doing as well in school as he would like. You think that he, too, is missing something that would allow him to roll ahead more smoothly. Identify the parts that he would need: additional effort on his part, tutoring support, an opportunity to talk over home-related problems with a resource person, or whatever might be appropriate in his case. The metaphor leaves you full latitude to offer the student any form of help and support that he may need.

PAPER, AN ERASER, AND A PENCIL

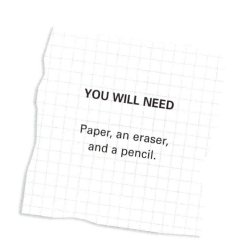

YOU WILL NEED

Paper, an eraser, and a pencil.

PURPOSE This technique will help students who take everything personally, or who find it hard to forgive others or themselves, to lighten their state of mind in order to leave some room for more agreeable thoughts.

INDIVIDUAL Ask the student to draw or scribble on one part of the paper, then on another, and yet another, until she has doodled over the entire page. Show her that, just as there is no space left on this sheet of paper for anything else, when she deliberately tries to remember everything (such as, anything she has been unable to do, all of her mistakes and all those that others have made etc.), it takes up all of her brain and leaves no room in it for anything else. So she needs to use a mental eraser to rub out any trace of her failures, hurts, and disappointments, so as to free her mind and regain the energy being wasted this way. By doing that, she will thereafter be able to think about more important things.

TIP

Saying only what is necessary

To sharpen the student's self-awareness in general, or with respect to special events.

To make the back-to-school moment easier after a long vacation, ask each student to summarize in a single word, number, sound, or gesture what he recalls about his long vacation. Although this is a short exercise, each student will have the impression that he shared some of his experience with the group and will be more apt to focus on tackling the new school day.

You can make optimal use of this exercise with a student who tends to get sidetracked when speaking before the class. By having him express the gist of his thoughts this way you will help him to attain the objective faster and learn how to better organize his thoughts.

87

Major Disruptions

The purpose of this technique is to make disruptive students who are constantly speaking and whispering in class realize that their behavior is really disturbing to others.

YOU WILL NEED

No supplies are needed for this technique.

●●● CLASS

Have the disruptive student stand in the center of the classroom. You will have previously assigned roles to the other members of the group so that they are prepared. Then you will ask them to form a circle around the troublemaker. On the count of three, each student will perform the task that you have assigned to him: to whisper, snigger, tell stories, walk away to look for an object, fidget constantly, and so on. In the meantime, you are standing slightly at a distance, presenting the day's lesson, which the student in the center must attempt to understand. Naturally, he will not be able to do it: he will then realize, because he has experienced it himself, how his behavior makes it hard for his classmates to pay attention.

●●● CLASS

You can vary the format of this exercise, for example, by designating just a few of the students as actors, while the others could be "observers" who will be making comments about what is going on. Depending upon how many troublemakers you have in your group, you could also direct more than one "disturbance" session at the same time. Do three students continually disturb the class? If so, divide the class into three subgroups of actors! The inevitable escalation of noise that will result will anchor the lesson even more deeply in the minds of the students concerned.

88

SWEETS

This technique will allow you to make the student understand the importance of increasing or reducing his "sweet" behaviors with others.

YOU WILL NEED

Sweets or baked treats (home-made or store-bought).

● INDIVIDUAL ●●● CLASS
The teacher gives the students some treats and asks them to describe how much they enjoy eating them. She then draws a parallel between this and the relationships among people, to underscore the point that some pleasant treats can be found there, too. The list of enjoyable things may include compliments made to someone who deserves them, kind and appreciative remarks, thank-you's, congratulations etc.

● INDIVIDUAL ●●● CLASS
In addition, you can elaborate on the negative aspects of the metaphor by stressing instead the harmful consequences of eating too many sweets: feeling nauseous or getting an upset stomach, the excessive weight gain, and other problems. Such consequences may be compared to the effects produced on others (teacher or friends) by someone who tries too hard to please: they soon feel nauseated, get fed up, and avoid him or criticize him (when they are not taking advantage of him). Therefore, it is important for us to keep the "sweets" we offer others in proportion, so that our actions retain their value and all of their good taste.

CONCLUSION

Douglas MacArthur said, "Youth is not a period of life, but an attitude of mind." I have seen teachers who had only been teaching for two years and were already old. They had lost their spark, were doing their work mechanically, had lost confidence in certain "problem cases" because of a lack of means to help them, and were no longer seeking new tools to make their classes more energizing and interesting. However, I have also known others whom I admire for their ability to maintain a truly youthful attitude in their profession, despite their twenty or thirty years of experience in the field. What distinguishes the latter from the others is that they are more popular with the students and their parents, as well as their colleagues. They are also happier on a daily basis: their work does not seem as oppressive to them because they have been learning and developing various strategies to adapt to the diversity of the student body that they are teaching. They know how to use the language of a smile and do their jobs with commitment and confidence. "Young" teachers are driven to constantly improve themselves and thus remain open to whatever is at all likely to enhance their skills—they are willing to take risks and try new methods and new techniques.

If you wish to stay young, you will need to do more than just read a book about the techniques you can use to help you in your work. You will also need to use them, adapt them to your students, and keep your interventions creative. Here, then, are a few simple suggestions to help you do this.

- **At the end of each school day, grade yourself from 0 to 10, to gauge your level of creativity with your students that day. You of all people know that any grade lower than "6" means you have failed!**

- **Every week, share with at least one of your colleagues something worthwhile that you accomplished with the entire class or with one student. If each person complies with this little rule, it will become contagious and you will all benefit from it.**

- **Go shopping in dollar stores. You will be amazed to discover all of the teaching materials that are sold there—and at cheap prices!**

- **Bring some of these one-dollar articles or other objects that you came across to your meetings with colleagues (or even with your students!) and, with their help, try to find ways of adapting them to your specific needs. Not only will you discover new tools among them, but you will also really enjoy doing this kind of exercise.**

BIBLIOGRAPHY

Beaulieu, Danie, *Techniques d'Impact pour grandir: illustrations pour développer l'intelligence émotionnelle chez les adolescents*, Lac-Beauport, Quebec: Éditions Académie Impact, 2000.

Gazzaniga, M. S., "The Split Brain Revisited", in *The Scientific American Book of the Brain*, edited by Anthony R. Damasio and the staff of *The Scientific American*, New York: Lyons Press, 1999.

Goleman, Daniel, *Emotional Intelligence: Why It Can Matter More than IQ*, New York: Bantam Books, 1995, translated by Thierry Piélat as *L'intelligence émotionnelle 1:* Comment *transformer ses émotions en intelligence*, Paris: Éditions Robert Laffont, 1997.

Peck, M. Scott, *The Road Less Traveled*, New York: Simon and Schuster, 1978, translated by Laurence Minard as *Le chemin le moins fréquenté*, Paris: Editions Robert Laffont, 1987.

Rossi, E.L., and Nimmons, D., *The Twenty-Minute Break: The Ultradian Healing Response*, Los Angeles: Zeig, Tucker & Co Inc, 1991.

Van der Kolk, Bessel, Alexander C. McFarlane, and Lars Weisaeth, *Traumatic Stress: the Effects of Overwhelming Experience on Mind, Body, and Society*, New York: The Guilford Press, 1996.